THE GOSPEL OF
LUKE

This edition of the ESV Gospel of Luke is published by
The Good Book Company 2017.
Reprinted 2019.

thegoodbook.com | www.thegoodbook.co.uk
thegoodbook.com.au | thegoodbook.co.nz | thegoodbook.co.in

ISBN: 9781784982737 | Printed in India.

Design by André Parker

THE GOSPEL OF

LUKE

Dedication to Theophilus

1 Inasmuch as many have undertaken to compile a narrative of the things that have been accomplished among us, ² just as those who from the beginning were eyewitnesses and ministers of the word have delivered them to us, ³ it seemed good to me also, having followed all things closely for some time past, to write an orderly account for you, most excellent Theophilus, ⁴ that you may have certainty concerning the things you have been taught.

Birth of John the Baptist Foretold

⁵ In the days of Herod, king of Judea, there was a priest named Zechariah, of the division of Abijah. And he had a wife from the daughters of Aaron, and her name was Elizabeth. ⁶ And they were both righteous before God, walking blamelessly in all the commandments and statutes of the Lord. ⁷ But they had no child, because Elizabeth was barren, and both were advanced in years.

⁸ Now while he was serving as priest before God when his division was on duty, ⁹ according to the custom of the priesthood, he was chosen by lot to enter the temple of the Lord and burn incense. ¹⁰ And the whole multitude of the people were praying outside at the hour of incense. ¹¹ And there appeared to him an angel of the Lord standing on the right side of the altar of incense. ¹² And Zechariah was troubled when he saw him, and fear fell upon him. ¹³ But the angel said to him, "Do not be afraid, Zechariah, for your prayer has been heard, and your wife Elizabeth will bear you a son, and you shall call his name John. ¹⁴ And you will have joy and gladness, and many will rejoice at his birth, ¹⁵ for he will be great before the Lord.

3

And he must not drink wine or strong drink, and he will be filled with the Holy Spirit, even from his mother's womb. [16] And he will turn many of the children of Israel to the Lord their God, [17] and he will go before him in the spirit and power of Elijah, to turn the hearts of the fathers to the children, and the disobedient to the wisdom of the just, to make ready for the Lord a people prepared."

[18] And Zechariah said to the angel, "How shall I know this? For I am an old man, and my wife is advanced in years." [19] And the angel answered him, "I am Gabriel. I stand in the presence of God, and I was sent to speak to you and to bring you this good news. [20] And behold, you will be silent and unable to speak until the day that these things take place, because you did not believe my words, which will be fulfilled in their time." [21] And the people were waiting for Zechariah, and they were wondering at his delay in the temple. [22] And when he came out, he was unable to speak to them, and they realized that he had seen a vision in the temple. And he kept making signs to them and remained mute. [23] And when his time of service was ended, he went to his home.

[24] After these days his wife Elizabeth conceived, and for five months she kept herself hidden, saying, [25] "Thus the Lord has done for me in the days when he looked on me, to take away my reproach among people."

Birth of Jesus Foretold

[26] In the sixth month the angel Gabriel was sent from God to a city of Galilee named Nazareth, [27] to a virgin betrothed to a man whose name was Joseph, of the house of David. And the virgin's name was Mary. [28] And he came to her and said, "Greetings, O favored one, the Lord is with you!" [29] But she was greatly troubled at the saying, and tried to discern what sort of greeting this might be. [30] And the angel said to her, "Do not be

afraid, Mary, for you have found favor with God. ³¹ And behold, you will conceive in your womb and bear a son, and you shall call his name Jesus. ³² He will be great and will be called the Son of the Most High. And the Lord God will give to him the throne of his father David, ³³ and he will reign over the house of Jacob forever, and of his kingdom there will be no end."

³⁴ And Mary said to the angel, "How will this be, since I am a virgin?"

³⁵ And the angel answered her, "The Holy Spirit will come upon you, and the power of the Most High will overshadow you; therefore the child to be born will be called holy—the Son of God. ³⁶ And behold, your relative Elizabeth in her old age has also conceived a son, and this is the sixth month with her who was called barren. ³⁷ For nothing will be impossible with God." ³⁸ And Mary said, "Behold, I am the servant of the Lord; let it be to me according to your word." And the angel departed from her.

Mary Visits Elizabeth

³⁹ In those days Mary arose and went with haste into the hill country, to a town in Judah, ⁴⁰ and she entered the house of Zechariah and greeted Elizabeth. ⁴¹ And when Elizabeth heard the greeting of Mary, the baby leaped in her womb. And Elizabeth was filled with the Holy Spirit, ⁴² and she exclaimed with a loud cry, "Blessed are you among women, and blessed is the fruit of your womb! ⁴³ And why is this granted to me that the mother of my Lord should come to me? ⁴⁴ For behold, when the sound of your greeting came to my ears, the baby in my womb leaped for joy. ⁴⁵ And blessed is she who believed that there would be a fulfillment of what was spoken to her from the Lord."

Mary's Song of Praise: The Magnificat

⁴⁶ And Mary said,

"My soul magnifies the Lord,
⁴⁷ and my spirit rejoices in God my Savior,
⁴⁸ for he has looked on
the humble estate of his servant.
For behold, from now on all generations
will call me blessed;
⁴⁹ for he who is mighty has done great things for me,
and holy is his name.
⁵⁰ And his mercy is for those who fear him
from generation to generation.
⁵¹ He has shown strength with his arm;
he has scattered the proud in the thoughts of
their hearts;
⁵² he has brought down the mighty from their thrones
and exalted those of humble estate;
⁵³ he has filled the hungry with good things,
and the rich he has sent away empty.
⁵⁴ He has helped his servant Israel,
in remembrance of his mercy,
⁵⁵ as he spoke to our fathers,
to Abraham and to his offspring forever."

⁵⁶ And Mary remained with her about three months and returned to her home.

The Birth of John the Baptist

⁵⁷ Now the time came for Elizabeth to give birth, and she bore a son. ⁵⁸ And her neighbors and relatives heard that the Lord had shown great mercy to her, and they rejoiced with her. ⁵⁹ And on the eighth day they came to circumcise the child. And they would have called him Zechariah after his father, ⁶⁰ but his

mother answered, "No; he shall be called John." ⁶¹ And they said to her, "None of your relatives is called by this name." ⁶² And they made signs to his father, inquiring what he wanted him to be called. ⁶³ And he asked for a writing tablet and wrote, "His name is John." And they all wondered. ⁶⁴ And immediately his mouth was opened and his tongue loosed, and he spoke, blessing God. ⁶⁵ And fear came on all their neighbors. And all these things were talked about through all the hill country of Judea, ⁶⁶ and all who heard them laid them up in their hearts, saying, "What then will this child be?" For the hand of the Lord was with him.

Zechariah's Prophecy

⁶⁷ And his father Zechariah was filled with the Holy Spirit and prophesied, saying,

⁶⁸ "Blessed be the Lord God of Israel,
    for he has visited and redeemed his people
⁶⁹ and has raised up a horn of salvation for us
    in the house of his servant David,
⁷⁰ as he spoke by the mouth of his holy prophets from of old,
⁷¹ that we should be saved from our enemies
    and from the hand of all who hate us;
⁷² to show the mercy promised to our fathers
    and to remember his holy covenant,
⁷³ the oath that he swore to our father Abraham, to grant us
⁷⁴ that we, being delivered from the hand of our enemies,
    might serve him without fear,
⁷⁵ in holiness and righteousness before him all our days.
⁷⁶ And you, child, will be called the prophet of the
    Most High;
    for you will go before the Lord to prepare his ways,
⁷⁷ to give knowledge of salvation to his people
    in the forgiveness of their sins,

⁷⁸ because of the tender mercy of our God,
>   whereby the sunrise shall visit us from on high
⁷⁹ to give light to those who sit in darkness and in
>   the shadow of death,
>   to guide our feet into the way of peace."

⁸⁰ And the child grew and became strong in spirit, and he was in the wilderness until the day of his public appearance to Israel.

The Birth of Jesus Christ

2 In those days a decree went out from Caesar Augustus that all the world should be registered. ² This was the first registration when Quirinius was governor of Syria. ³ And all went to be registered, each to his own town. ⁴ And Joseph also went up from Galilee, from the town of Nazareth, to Judea, to the city of David, which is called Bethlehem, because he was of the house and lineage of David, ⁵ to be registered with Mary, his betrothed, who was with child. ⁶ And while they were there, the time came for her to give birth. ⁷ And she gave birth to her firstborn son and wrapped him in swaddling cloths and laid him in a manger, because there was no place for them in the inn.

The Shepherds and the Angels

⁸ And in the same region there were shepherds out in the field, keeping watch over their flock by night. ⁹ And an angel of the Lord appeared to them, and the glory of the Lord shone around them, and they were filled with great fear. ¹⁰ And the angel said to them, "Fear not, for behold, I bring you good news of great joy that will be for all the people. ¹¹ For unto you is born this day in the city of David a Savior, who is Christ the Lord. ¹² And this will be a sign for you: you will find a baby wrapped in swaddling cloths and lying in a manger." ¹³ And suddenly there was with the angel a multitude of the heavenly host praising God and saying,

¹⁴ "Glory to God in the highest,
and on earth peace among those with
whom he is pleased!"

¹⁵ When the angels went away from them into heaven, the shepherds said to one another, "Let us go over to Bethlehem and see this thing that has happened, which the Lord has made known to us." ¹⁶ And they went with haste and found Mary and Joseph, and the baby lying in a manger. ¹⁷ And when they saw it, they made known the saying that had been told them concerning this child. ¹⁸ And all who heard it wondered at what the shepherds told them. ¹⁹ But Mary treasured up all these things, pondering them in her heart. ²⁰ And the shepherds returned, glorifying and praising God for all they had heard and seen, as it had been told them.

²¹ And at the end of eight days, when he was circumcised, he was called Jesus, the name given by the angel before he was conceived in the womb.

Jesus Presented at the Temple

²² And when the time came for their purification according to the Law of Moses, they brought him up to Jerusalem to present him to the Lord ²³ (as it is written in the Law of the Lord, "Every male who first opens the womb shall be called holy to the Lord") ²⁴ and to offer a sacrifice according to what is said in the Law of the Lord, "a pair of turtledoves, or two young pigeons." ²⁵ Now there was a man in Jerusalem, whose name was Simeon, and this man was righteous and devout, waiting for the consolation of Israel, and the Holy Spirit was upon him. ²⁶ And it had been revealed to him by the Holy Spirit that he would not see death before he had seen the Lord's Christ. ²⁷ And he came in the Spirit into the temple, and when the parents brought in the child Jesus, to do for him according to the custom of the Law, ²⁸ he took him up in his arms and blessed God and said,

²⁹ "Lord, now you are letting your servant depart in peace,
according to your word;
³⁰ for my eyes have seen your salvation
³¹ that you have prepared in the presence of all peoples,
³² a light for revelation to the Gentiles,
and for glory to your people Israel."

³³ And his father and his mother marveled at what was said about him. ³⁴ And Simeon blessed them and said to Mary his mother, "Behold, this child is appointed for the fall and rising of many in Israel, and for a sign that is opposed ³⁵ (and a sword will pierce through your own soul also), so that thoughts from many hearts may be revealed."

³⁶ And there was a prophetess, Anna, the daughter of Phanuel, of the tribe of Asher. She was advanced in years, having lived with her husband seven years from when she was a virgin, ³⁷ and then as a widow until she was eighty-four. She did not depart from the temple, worshiping with fasting and prayer night and day. ³⁸ And coming up at that very hour she began to give thanks to God and to speak of him to all who were waiting for the redemption of Jerusalem.

The Return to Nazareth

³⁹ And when they had performed everything according to the Law of the Lord, they returned into Galilee, to their own town of Nazareth. ⁴⁰ And the child grew and became strong, filled with wisdom. And the favor of God was upon him.

The Boy Jesus in the Temple

⁴¹ Now his parents went to Jerusalem every year at the Feast of the Passover. ⁴² And when he was twelve years old, they went up according to custom. ⁴³ And when the feast was ended, as they were returning, the boy Jesus stayed behind in Jerusalem. His parents did not know it, ⁴⁴ but supposing him to be in the

group they went a day's journey, but then they began to search for him among their relatives and acquaintances, ⁴⁵ and when they did not find him, they returned to Jerusalem, searching for him. ⁴⁶ After three days they found him in the temple, sitting among the teachers, listening to them and asking them questions. ⁴⁷ And all who heard him were amazed at his understanding and his answers. ⁴⁸ And when his parents saw him, they were astonished. And his mother said to him, "Son, why have you treated us so? Behold, your father and I have been searching for you in great distress." ⁴⁹ And he said to them, "Why were you looking for me? Did you not know that I must be in my Father's house?" ⁵⁰ And they did not understand the saying that he spoke to them. ⁵¹ And he went down with them and came to Nazareth and was submissive to them. And his mother treasured up all these things in her heart.

⁵² And Jesus increased in wisdom and in stature and in favor with God and man.

John the Baptist Prepares the Way

3 In the fifteenth year of the reign of Tiberius Caesar, Pontius Pilate being governor of Judea, and Herod being tetrarch of Galilee, and his brother Philip tetrarch of the region of Ituraea and Trachonitis, and Lysanias tetrarch of Abilene, ² during the high priesthood of Annas and Caiaphas, the word of God came to John the son of Zechariah in the wilderness. ³ And he went into all the region around the Jordan, proclaiming a baptism of repentance for the forgiveness of sins. ⁴ As it is written in the book of the words of Isaiah the prophet,

"The voice of one crying in the wilderness:
    'Prepare the way of the Lord,
        make his paths straight.
    ⁵ Every valley shall be filled,
        and every mountain and hill shall be made low,

11

and the crooked shall become straight,
and the rough places shall become level ways,
⁶ and all flesh shall see the salvation of God.'"

⁷ He said therefore to the crowds that came out to be baptized by him, "You brood of vipers! Who warned you to flee from the wrath to come? ⁸ Bear fruits in keeping with repentance. And do not begin to say to yourselves, 'We have Abraham as our father.' For I tell you, God is able from these stones to raise up children for Abraham. ⁹ Even now the axe is laid to the root of the trees. Every tree therefore that does not bear good fruit is cut down and thrown into the fire."

¹⁰ And the crowds asked him, "What then shall we do?" ¹¹ And he answered them, "Whoever has two tunics is to share with him who has none, and whoever has food is to do likewise." ¹² Tax collectors also came to be baptized and said to him, "Teacher, what shall we do?" ¹³ And he said to them, "Collect no more than you are authorized to do." ¹⁴ Soldiers also asked him, "And we, what shall we do?" And he said to them, "Do not extort money from anyone by threats or by false accusation, and be content with your wages."

¹⁵ As the people were in expectation, and all were questioning in their hearts concerning John, whether he might be the Christ, ¹⁶ John answered them all, saying, "I baptize you with water, but he who is mightier than I is coming, the strap of whose sandals I am not worthy to untie. He will baptize you with the Holy Spirit and fire. ¹⁷ His winnowing fork is in his hand, to clear his threshing floor and to gather the wheat into his barn, but the chaff he will burn with unquenchable fire."

¹⁸ So with many other exhortations he preached good news to the people. ¹⁹ But Herod the tetrarch, who had been reproved by him for Herodias, his brother's wife, and for all the evil things that Herod had done, ²⁰ added this to them all, that he locked up John in prison.

²¹ Now when all the people were baptized, and when Jesus also had been baptized and was praying, the heavens were opened, ²² and the Holy Spirit descended on him in bodily form, like a dove; and a voice came from heaven, "You are my beloved Son; with you I am well pleased."

The Genealogy of Jesus Christ

²³ Jesus, when he began his ministry, was about thirty years of age, being the son (as was supposed) of Joseph, the son of Heli, ²⁴ the son of Matthat, the son of Levi, the son of Melchi, the son of Jannai, the son of Joseph, ²⁵ the son of Mattathias, the son of Amos, the son of Nahum, the son of Esli, the son of Naggai, ²⁶ the son of Maath, the son of Mattathias, the son of Semein, the son of Josech, the son of Joda, ²⁷ the son of Joanan, the son of Rhesa, the son of Zerubbabel, the son of Shealtiel, the son of Neri, ²⁸ the son of Melchi, the son of Addi, the son of Cosam, the son of Elmadam, the son of Er, ²⁹ the son of Joshua, the son of Eliezer, the son of Jorim, the son of Matthat, the son of Levi, ³⁰ the son of Simeon, the son of Judah, the son of Joseph, the son of Jonam, the son of Eliakim, ³¹ the son of Melea, the son of Menna, the son of Mattatha, the son of Nathan, the son of David, ³² the son of Jesse, the son of Obed, the son of Boaz, the son of Sala, the son of Nahshon, ³³ the son of Amminadab, the son of Admin, the son of Arni, the son of Hezron, the son of Perez, the son of Judah, ³⁴ the son of Jacob, the son of Isaac, the son of Abraham, the son of Terah, the son of Nahor, ³⁵ the son of Serug, the son of Reu, the son of Peleg, the son of Eber, the son of Shelah, ³⁶ the son of Cainan, the son of Arphaxad, the son of Shem, the son of Noah, the son of Lamech, ³⁷ the son of Methuselah, the son of Enoch, the son of Jared, the son of Mahalaleel, the son of Cainan, ³⁸ the son of Enos, the son of Seth, the son of Adam, the son of God.

The Temptation of Jesus

4 And Jesus, full of the Holy Spirit, returned from the Jordan and was led by the Spirit in the wilderness ² for forty days, being tempted by the devil. And he ate nothing during those days. And when they were ended, he was hungry. ³ The devil said to him, "If you are the Son of God, command this stone to become bread." ⁴ And Jesus answered him, "It is written, 'Man shall not live by bread alone.'" ⁵ And the devil took him up and showed him all the kingdoms of the world in a moment of time, ⁶ and said to him, "To you I will give all this authority and their glory, for it has been delivered to me, and I give it to whom I will. ⁷ If you, then, will worship me, it will all be yours." ⁸ And Jesus answered him, "It is written,

> "'You shall worship the Lord your God,
>   and him only shall you serve.'"

⁹ And he took him to Jerusalem and set him on the pinnacle of the temple and said to him, "If you are the Son of God, throw yourself down from here, ¹⁰ for it is written,

> "'He will command his angels concerning you,
>   to guard you,'

¹¹ and

> "'On their hands they will bear you up,
>   lest you strike your foot against a stone.'"

¹² And Jesus answered him, "It is said, 'You shall not put the Lord your God to the test.'" ¹³ And when the devil had ended every temptation, he departed from him until an opportune time.

Jesus Begins His Ministry

¹⁴ And Jesus returned in the power of the Spirit to Galilee, and a report about him went out through all the surrounding country. ¹⁵ And he taught in their synagogues, being glorified by all.

Jesus Rejected at Nazareth

16 And he came to Nazareth, where he had been brought up. And as was his custom, he went to the synagogue on the Sabbath day, and he stood up to read. 17 And the scroll of the prophet Isaiah was given to him. He unrolled the scroll and found the place where it was written,

> 18 "The Spirit of the Lord is upon me,
>> because he has anointed me
>> to proclaim good news to the poor.
> He has sent me to proclaim liberty to the captives
>> and recovering of sight to the blind,
>> to set at liberty those who are oppressed,
> 19 to proclaim the year of the Lord's favor."

20 And he rolled up the scroll and gave it back to the attendant and sat down. And the eyes of all in the synagogue were fixed on him. 21 And he began to say to them, "Today this Scripture has been fulfilled in your hearing." 22 And all spoke well of him and marveled at the gracious words that were coming from his mouth. And they said, "Is not this Joseph's son?" 23 And he said to them, "Doubtless you will quote to me this proverb, '"Physician, heal yourself." What we have heard you did at Capernaum, do here in your hometown as well.'" 24 And he said, "Truly, I say to you, no prophet is acceptable in his hometown. 25 But in truth, I tell you, there were many widows in Israel in the days of Elijah, when the heavens were shut up three years and six months, and a great famine came over all the land, 26 and Elijah was sent to none of them but only to Zarephath, in the land of Sidon, to a woman who was a widow. 27 And there were many lepers in Israel in the time of the prophet Elisha, and none of them was cleansed, but only Naaman the Syrian." 28 When they heard these things, all in the synagogue were filled with wrath. 29 And they rose up and drove him out of the town and brought him to the brow of the hill on which their town was

built, so that they could throw him down the cliff. ³⁰ But passing through their midst, he went away.

Jesus Heals a Man with an Unclean Demon

³¹ And he went down to Capernaum, a city of Galilee. And he was teaching them on the Sabbath, ³² and they were astonished at his teaching, for his word possessed authority. ³³ And in the synagogue there was a man who had the spirit of an unclean demon, and he cried out with a loud voice, ³⁴ "Ha! What have you to do with us, Jesus of Nazareth? Have you come to destroy us? I know who you are—the Holy One of God." ³⁵ But Jesus rebuked him, saying, "Be silent and come out of him!" And when the demon had thrown him down in their midst, he came out of him, having done him no harm. ³⁶ And they were all amazed and said to one another, "What is this word? For with authority and power he commands the unclean spirits, and they come out!" ³⁷ And reports about him went out into every place in the surrounding region.

Jesus Heals Many

³⁸ And he arose and left the synagogue and entered Simon's house. Now Simon's mother-in-law was ill with a high fever, and they appealed to him on her behalf. ³⁹ And he stood over her and rebuked the fever, and it left her, and immediately she rose and began to serve them.

⁴⁰ Now when the sun was setting, all those who had any who were sick with various diseases brought them to him, and he laid his hands on every one of them and healed them. ⁴¹ And demons also came out of many, crying, "You are the Son of God!" But he rebuked them and would not allow them to speak, because they knew that he was the Christ.

Jesus Preaches in Synagogues

⁴² And when it was day, he departed and went into a desolate place. And the people sought him and came to him, and would have kept him from leaving them, ⁴³ but he said to them, "I must preach the good news of the kingdom of God to the other towns as well; for I was sent for this purpose." ⁴⁴ And he was preaching in the synagogues of Judea.

Jesus Calls the First Disciples

5 On one occasion, while the crowd was pressing in on him to hear the word of God, he was standing by the lake of Gennesaret, ² and he saw two boats by the lake, but the fishermen had gone out of them and were washing their nets. ³ Getting into one of the boats, which was Simon's, he asked him to put out a little from the land. And he sat down and taught the people from the boat. ⁴ And when he had finished speaking, he said to Simon, "Put out into the deep and let down your nets for a catch." ⁵ And Simon answered, "Master, we toiled all night and took nothing! But at your word I will let down the nets." ⁶ And when they had done this, they enclosed a large number of fish, and their nets were breaking. ⁷ They signaled to their partners in the other boat to come and help them. And they came and filled both the boats, so that they began to sink. ⁸ But when Simon Peter saw it, he fell down at Jesus' knees, saying, "Depart from me, for I am a sinful man, O Lord." ⁹ For he and all who were with him were astonished at the catch of fish that they had taken, ¹⁰ and so also were James and John, sons of Zebedee, who were partners with Simon. And Jesus said to Simon, "Do not be afraid; from now on you will be catching men." ¹¹ And when they had brought their boats to land, they left everything and followed him.

Jesus Cleanses a Leper

[12] While he was in one of the cities, there came a man full of leprosy. And when he saw Jesus, he fell on his face and begged him, "Lord, if you will, you can make me clean." [13] And Jesus stretched out his hand and touched him, saying, "I will; be clean." And immediately the leprosy left him. [14] And he charged him to tell no one, but "go and show yourself to the priest, and make an offering for your cleansing, as Moses commanded, for a proof to them." [15] But now even more the report about him went abroad, and great crowds gathered to hear him and to be healed of their infirmities. [16] But he would withdraw to desolate places and pray.

Jesus Heals a Paralytic

[17] On one of those days, as he was teaching, Pharisees and teachers of the law were sitting there, who had come from every village of Galilee and Judea and from Jerusalem. And the power of the Lord was with him to heal. [18] And behold, some men were bringing on a bed a man who was paralyzed, and they were seeking to bring him in and lay him before Jesus, [19] but finding no way to bring him in, because of the crowd, they went up on the roof and let him down with his bed through the tiles into the midst before Jesus. [20] And when he saw their faith, he said, "Man, your sins are forgiven you." [21] And the scribes and the Pharisees began to question, saying, "Who is this who speaks blasphemies? Who can forgive sins but God alone?" [22] When Jesus perceived their thoughts, he answered them, "Why do you question in your hearts? [23] Which is easier, to say, 'Your sins are forgiven you,' or to say, 'Rise and walk'? [24] But that you may know that the Son of Man has authority on earth to forgive sins"—he said to the man who was paralyzed—"I say to you, rise, pick up your bed and go home." [25] And immediately he rose up before them and picked up what he had been lying on and

went home, glorifying God. ²⁶ And amazement seized them all, and they glorified God and were filled with awe, saying, "We have seen extraordinary things today."

Jesus Calls Levi

²⁷ After this he went out and saw a tax collector named Levi, sitting at the tax booth. And he said to him, "Follow me." ²⁸ And leaving everything, he rose and followed him.

²⁹ And Levi made him a great feast in his house, and there was a large company of tax collectors and others reclining at table with them. ³⁰ And the Pharisees and their scribes grumbled at his disciples, saying, "Why do you eat and drink with tax collectors and sinners?" ³¹ And Jesus answered them, "Those who are well have no need of a physician, but those who are sick. ³² I have not come to call the righteous but sinners to repentance."

A Question About Fasting

³³ And they said to him, "The disciples of John fast often and offer prayers, and so do the disciples of the Pharisees, but yours eat and drink." ³⁴ And Jesus said to them, "Can you make wedding guests fast while the bridegroom is with them? ³⁵ The days will come when the bridegroom is taken away from them, and then they will fast in those days." ³⁶ He also told them a parable: "No one tears a piece from a new garment and puts it on an old garment. If he does, he will tear the new, and the piece from the new will not match the old. ³⁷ And no one puts new wine into old wineskins. If he does, the new wine will burst the skins and it will be spilled, and the skins will be destroyed. ³⁸ But new wine must be put into fresh wineskins. ³⁹ And no one after drinking old wine desires new, for he says, 'The old is good.'"

Jesus Is Lord of the Sabbath

6 On a Sabbath, while he was going through the grainfields, his disciples plucked and ate some heads of grain, rubbing them in their hands. ² But some of the Pharisees said, "Why are you doing what is not lawful to do on the Sabbath?" ³ And Jesus answered them, "Have you not read what David did when he was hungry, he and those who were with him: ⁴ how he entered the house of God and took and ate the bread of the Presence, which is not lawful for any but the priests to eat, and also gave it to those with him?" ⁵ And he said to them, "The Son of Man is lord of the Sabbath."

A Man with a Withered Hand

⁶ On another Sabbath, he entered the synagogue and was teaching, and a man was there whose right hand was withered. ⁷ And the scribes and the Pharisees watched him, to see whether he would heal on the Sabbath, so that they might find a reason to accuse him. ⁸ But he knew their thoughts, and he said to the man with the withered hand, "Come and stand here." And he rose and stood there. ⁹ And Jesus said to them, "I ask you, is it lawful on the Sabbath to do good or to do harm, to save life or to destroy it?" ¹⁰ And after looking around at them all he said to him, "Stretch out your hand." And he did so, and his hand was restored. ¹¹ But they were filled with fury and discussed with one another what they might do to Jesus.

The Twelve Apostles

¹² In these days he went out to the mountain to pray, and all night he continued in prayer to God. ¹³ And when day came, he called his disciples and chose from them twelve, whom he named apostles: ¹⁴ Simon, whom he named Peter, and Andrew his brother, and James and John, and Philip, and Bartholomew, ¹⁵ and Matthew, and Thomas, and James the son of Alphaeus,

and Simon who was called the Zealot, [16] and Judas the son of James, and Judas Iscariot, who became a traitor.

Jesus Ministers to a Great Multitude

[17] And he came down with them and stood on a level place, with a great crowd of his disciples and a great multitude of people from all Judea and Jerusalem and the seacoast of Tyre and Sidon, [18] who came to hear him and to be healed of their diseases. And those who were troubled with unclean spirits were cured. [19] And all the crowd sought to touch him, for power came out from him and healed them all.

The Beatitudes

[20] And he lifted up his eyes on his disciples, and said:

"Blessed are you who are poor,
for yours is the kingdom of God.
[21] "Blessed are you who are hungry now,
for you shall be satisfied.

"Blessed are you who weep now,
for you shall laugh.
[22] "Blessed are you when people hate you
and when they exclude you and revile you
and spurn your name as evil,
on account of the Son of Man!
[23] Rejoice in that day, and leap for joy,
for behold, your reward is great in heaven;
for so their fathers did to the prophets.

Jesus Pronounces Woes

[24] "But woe to you who are rich,
for you have received your consolation.
[25] "Woe to you who are full now,
for you shall be hungry.

"Woe to you who laugh now,
for you shall mourn and weep.
²⁶ "Woe to you, when all people speak well of you,
for so their fathers did to the false prophets.

Love Your Enemies

²⁷ "But I say to you who hear, Love your enemies, do good to those who hate you, ²⁸ bless those who curse you, pray for those who abuse you. ²⁹ To one who strikes you on the cheek, offer the other also, and from one who takes away your cloak do not withhold your tunic either. ³⁰ Give to everyone who begs from you, and from one who takes away your goods do not demand them back. ³¹ And as you wish that others would do to you, do so to them.

³² "If you love those who love you, what benefit is that to you? For even sinners love those who love them. ³³ And if you do good to those who do good to you, what benefit is that to you? For even sinners do the same. ³⁴ And if you lend to those from whom you expect to receive, what credit is that to you? Even sinners lend to sinners, to get back the same amount. ³⁵ But love your enemies, and do good, and lend, expecting nothing in return, and your reward will be great, and you will be sons of the Most High, for he is kind to the ungrateful and the evil. ³⁶ Be merciful, even as your Father is merciful.

Judging Others

³⁷ "Judge not, and you will not be judged; condemn not, and you will not be condemned; forgive, and you will be forgiven; ³⁸ give, and it will be given to you. Good measure, pressed down, shaken together, running over, will be put into your lap. For with the measure you use it will be measured back to you."

³⁹ He also told them a parable: "Can a blind man lead a blind man? Will they not both fall into a pit? ⁴⁰ A disciple is not above

his teacher, but everyone when he is fully trained will be like his teacher. ⁴¹ Why do you see the speck that is in your brother's eye, but do not notice the log that is in your own eye? ⁴² How can you say to your brother, 'Brother, let me take out the speck that is in your eye,' when you yourself do not see the log that is in your own eye? You hypocrite, first take the log out of your own eye, and then you will see clearly to take out the speck that is in your brother's eye.

A Tree and Its Fruit

⁴³ "For no good tree bears bad fruit, nor again does a bad tree bear good fruit, ⁴⁴ for each tree is known by its own fruit. For figs are not gathered from thornbushes, nor are grapes picked from a bramble bush. ⁴⁵ The good person out of the good treasure of his heart produces good, and the evil person out of his evil treasure produces evil, for out of the abundance of the heart his mouth speaks.

Build Your House on the Rock

⁴⁶ "Why do you call me 'Lord, Lord,' and not do what I tell you? ⁴⁷ Everyone who comes to me and hears my words and does them, I will show you what he is like: ⁴⁸ he is like a man building a house, who dug deep and laid the foundation on the rock. And when a flood arose, the stream broke against that house and could not shake it, because it had been well built. ⁴⁹ But the one who hears and does not do them is like a man who built a house on the ground without a foundation. When the stream broke against it, immediately it fell, and the ruin of that house was great."

Jesus Heals a Centurion's Servant

7 After he had finished all his sayings in the hearing of the people, he entered Capernaum. ² Now a centurion had a

servant who was sick and at the point of death, who was highly valued by him. ³ When the centurion heard about Jesus, he sent to him elders of the Jews, asking him to come and heal his servant. ⁴ And when they came to Jesus, they pleaded with him earnestly, saying, "He is worthy to have you do this for him, ⁵ for he loves our nation, and he is the one who built us our synagogue." ⁶ And Jesus went with them. When he was not far from the house, the centurion sent friends, saying to him, "Lord, do not trouble yourself, for I am not worthy to have you come under my roof. ⁷ Therefore I did not presume to come to you. But say the word, and let my servant be healed. ⁸ For I too am a man set under authority, with soldiers under me: and I say to one, 'Go,' and he goes; and to another, 'Come,' and he comes; and to my servant, 'Do this,' and he does it." ⁹ When Jesus heard these things, he marveled at him, and turning to the crowd that followed him, said, "I tell you, not even in Israel have I found such faith." ¹⁰ And when those who had been sent returned to the house, they found the servant well.

Jesus Raises a Widow's Son

¹¹ Soon afterward he went to a town called Nain, and his disciples and a great crowd went with him. ¹² As he drew near to the gate of the town, behold, a man who had died was being carried out, the only son of his mother, and she was a widow, and a considerable crowd from the town was with her. ¹³ And when the Lord saw her, he had compassion on her and said to her, "Do not weep." ¹⁴ Then he came up and touched the bier, and the bearers stood still. And he said, "Young man, I say to you, arise." ¹⁵ And the dead man sat up and began to speak, and Jesus gave him to his mother. ¹⁶ Fear seized them all, and they glorified God, saying, "A great prophet has arisen among us!" and "God has visited his people!" ¹⁷ And this report about him spread through the whole of Judea and all the surrounding country.

Messengers from John the Baptist

¹⁸ The disciples of John reported all these things to him. And John, ¹⁹ calling two of his disciples to him, sent them to the Lord, saying, "Are you the one who is to come, or shall we look for another?" ²⁰ And when the men had come to him, they said, "John the Baptist has sent us to you, saying, 'Are you the one who is to come, or shall we look for another?'" ²¹ In that hour he healed many people of diseases and plagues and evil spirits, and on many who were blind he bestowed sight. ²² And he answered them, "Go and tell John what you have seen and heard: the blind receive their sight, the lame walk, lepers are cleansed, and the deaf hear, the dead are raised up, the poor have good news preached to them. ²³ And blessed is the one who is not offended by me."

²⁴ When John's messengers had gone, Jesus began to speak to the crowds concerning John: "What did you go out into the wilderness to see? A reed shaken by the wind? ²⁵ What then did you go out to see? A man dressed in soft clothing? Behold, those who are dressed in splendid clothing and live in luxury are in kings' courts. ²⁶ What then did you go out to see? A prophet? Yes, I tell you, and more than a prophet. ²⁷ This is he of whom it is written,

"'Behold, I send my messenger before your face,
    who will prepare your way before you.'

²⁸ I tell you, among those born of women none is greater than John. Yet the one who is least in the kingdom of God is greater than he." ²⁹ (When all the people heard this, and the tax collectors too, they declared God just, having been baptized with the baptism of John, ³⁰ but the Pharisees and the lawyers rejected the purpose of God for themselves, not having been baptized by him.)

³¹ "To what then shall I compare the people of this generation, and what are they like? ³² They are like children sitting in the marketplace and calling to one another,

"'We played the flute for you, and you did not dance;
we sang a dirge, and you did not weep.'

[33] For John the Baptist has come eating no bread and drinking no wine, and you say, 'He has a demon.' [34] The Son of Man has come eating and drinking, and you say, 'Look at him! A glutton and a drunkard, a friend of tax collectors and sinners!' [35] Yet wisdom is justified by all her children."

A Sinful Woman Forgiven

[36] One of the Pharisees asked him to eat with him, and he went into the Pharisee's house and reclined at table. [37] And behold, a woman of the city, who was a sinner, when she learned that he was reclining at table in the Pharisee's house, brought an alabaster flask of ointment, [38] and standing behind him at his feet, weeping, she began to wet his feet with her tears and wiped them with the hair of her head and kissed his feet and anointed them with the ointment. [39] Now when the Pharisee who had invited him saw this, he said to himself, "If this man were a prophet, he would have known who and what sort of woman this is who is touching him, for she is a sinner." [40] And Jesus answering said to him, "Simon, I have something to say to you." And he answered, "Say it, Teacher."

[41] "A certain moneylender had two debtors. One owed five hundred denarii, and the other fifty. [42] When they could not pay, he cancelled the debt of both. Now which of them will love him more?" [43] Simon answered, "The one, I suppose, for whom he cancelled the larger debt." And he said to him, "You have judged rightly." [44] Then turning toward the woman he said to Simon, "Do you see this woman? I entered your house; you gave me no water for my feet, but she has wet my feet with her tears and wiped them with her hair. [45] You gave me no kiss, but from the time I came in she has not ceased to kiss my feet. [46] You did not anoint my head with oil, but she has anointed my feet with

ointment. ⁴⁷ Therefore I tell you, her sins, which are many, are forgiven—for she loved much. But he who is forgiven little, loves little." ⁴⁸ And he said to her, "Your sins are forgiven." ⁴⁹ Then those who were at table with him began to say among themselves, "Who is this, who even forgives sins?" ⁵⁰ And he said to the woman, "Your faith has saved you; go in peace."

Women Accompanying Jesus

8 Soon afterward he went on through cities and villages, proclaiming and bringing the good news of the kingdom of God. And the twelve were with him, ² and also some women who had been healed of evil spirits and infirmities: Mary, called Magdalene, from whom seven demons had gone out, ³ and Joanna, the wife of Chuza, Herod's household manager, and Susanna, and many others, who provided for them out of their means.

The Parable of the Sower

⁴ And when a great crowd was gathering and people from town after town came to him, he said in a parable, ⁵ "A sower went out to sow his seed. And as he sowed, some fell along the path and was trampled underfoot, and the birds of the air devoured it. ⁶ And some fell on the rock, and as it grew up, it withered away, because it had no moisture. ⁷ And some fell among thorns, and the thorns grew up with it and choked it. ⁸ And some fell into good soil and grew and yielded a hundredfold." As he said these things, he called out, "He who has ears to hear, let him hear."

The Purpose of the Parables

⁹ And when his disciples asked him what this parable meant, ¹⁰ he said, "To you it has been given to know the secrets of the kingdom of God, but for others they are in parables, so that 'seeing they may not see, and hearing they may not understand.'

[11] Now the parable is this: The seed is the word of God. [12] The ones along the path are those who have heard; then the devil comes and takes away the word from their hearts, so that they may not believe and be saved. [13] And the ones on the rock are those who, when they hear the word, receive it with joy. But these have no root; they believe for a while, and in time of testing fall away. [14] And as for what fell among the thorns, they are those who hear, but as they go on their way they are choked by the cares and riches and pleasures of life, and their fruit does not mature. [15] As for that in the good soil, they are those who, hearing the word, hold it fast in an honest and good heart, and bear fruit with patience.

A Lamp Under a Jar

[16] "No one after lighting a lamp covers it with a jar or puts it under a bed, but puts it on a stand, so that those who enter may see the light. [17] For nothing is hidden that will not be made manifest, nor is anything secret that will not be known and come to light. [18] Take care then how you hear, for to the one who has, more will be given, and from the one who has not, even what he thinks that he has will be taken away."

Jesus' Mother and Brothers

[19] Then his mother and his brothers came to him, but they could not reach him because of the crowd. [20] And he was told, "Your mother and your brothers are standing outside, desiring to see you." [21] But he answered them, "My mother and my brothers are those who hear the word of God and do it."

Jesus Calms a Storm

[22] One day he got into a boat with his disciples, and he said to them, "Let us go across to the other side of the lake." So they set out, [23] and as they sailed he fell asleep. And a windstorm came

down on the lake, and they were filling with water and were in danger. ²⁴ And they went and woke him, saying, "Master, Master, we are perishing!" And he awoke and rebuked the wind and the raging waves, and they ceased, and there was a calm. ²⁵ He said to them, "Where is your faith?" And they were afraid, and they marveled, saying to one another, "Who then is this, that he commands even winds and water, and they obey him?"

Jesus Heals a Man with a Demon

²⁶ Then they sailed to the country of the Gerasenes, which is opposite Galilee. ²⁷ When Jesus had stepped out on land, there met him a man from the city who had demons. For a long time he had worn no clothes, and he had not lived in a house but among the tombs. ²⁸ When he saw Jesus, he cried out and fell down before him and said with a loud voice, "What have you to do with me, Jesus, Son of the Most High God? I beg you, do not torment me." ²⁹ For he had commanded the unclean spirit to come out of the man. (For many a time it had seized him. He was kept under guard and bound with chains and shackles, but he would break the bonds and be driven by the demon into the desert.) ³⁰ Jesus then asked him, "What is your name?" And he said, "Legion," for many demons had entered him. ³¹ And they begged him not to command them to depart into the abyss. ³² Now a large herd of pigs was feeding there on the hillside, and they begged him to let them enter these. So he gave them permission. ³³ Then the demons came out of the man and entered the pigs, and the herd rushed down the steep bank into the lake and drowned.

³⁴ When the herdsmen saw what had happened, they fled and told it in the city and in the country. ³⁵ Then people went out to see what had happened, and they came to Jesus and found the man from whom the demons had gone, sitting at the feet of Jesus, clothed and in his right mind, and they were afraid. ³⁶ And those who had seen it told them how the demon-possessed

man had been healed. [37] Then all the people of the surrounding country of the Gerasenes asked him to depart from them, for they were seized with great fear. So he got into the boat and returned. [38] The man from whom the demons had gone begged that he might be with him, but Jesus sent him away, saying, [39] "Return to your home, and declare how much God has done for you." And he went away, proclaiming throughout the whole city how much Jesus had done for him.

Jesus Heals a Woman and Jairus's Daughter

[40] Now when Jesus returned, the crowd welcomed him, for they were all waiting for him. [41] And there came a man named Jairus, who was a ruler of the synagogue. And falling at Jesus' feet, he implored him to come to his house, [42] for he had an only daughter, about twelve years of age, and she was dying.

As Jesus went, the people pressed around him. [43] And there was a woman who had had a discharge of blood for twelve years, and though she had spent all her living on physicians, she could not be healed by anyone. [44] She came up behind him and touched the fringe of his garment, and immediately her discharge of blood ceased. [45] And Jesus said, "Who was it that touched me?" When all denied it, Peter said, "Master, the crowds surround you and are pressing in on you!" [46] But Jesus said, "Someone touched me, for I perceive that power has gone out from me." [47] And when the woman saw that she was not hidden, she came trembling, and falling down before him declared in the presence of all the people why she had touched him, and how she had been immediately healed. [48] And he said to her, "Daughter, your faith has made you well; go in peace."

[49] While he was still speaking, someone from the ruler's house came and said, "Your daughter is dead; do not trouble the Teacher any more." [50] But Jesus on hearing this answered him, "Do not fear; only believe, and she will be well." [51] And when

he came to the house, he allowed no one to enter with him, except Peter and John and James, and the father and mother of the child. ⁵² And all were weeping and mourning for her, but he said, "Do not weep, for she is not dead but sleeping." ⁵³ And they laughed at him, knowing that she was dead. ⁵⁴ But taking her by the hand he called, saying, "Child, arise." ⁵⁵ And her spirit returned, and she got up at once. And he directed that something should be given her to eat. ⁵⁶ And her parents were amazed, but he charged them to tell no one what had happened.

Jesus Sends Out the Twelve Apostles

9 And he called the twelve together and gave them power and authority over all demons and to cure diseases, ² and he sent them out to proclaim the kingdom of God and to heal. ³ And he said to them, "Take nothing for your journey, no staff, nor bag, nor bread, nor money; and do not have two tunics. ⁴ And whatever house you enter, stay there, and from there depart. ⁵ And wherever they do not receive you, when you leave that town shake off the dust from your feet as a testimony against them." ⁶ And they departed and went through the villages, preaching the gospel and healing everywhere.

Herod Is Perplexed by Jesus

⁷ Now Herod the tetrarch heard about all that was happening, and he was perplexed, because it was said by some that John had been raised from the dead, ⁸ by some that Elijah had appeared, and by others that one of the prophets of old had risen. ⁹ Herod said, "John I beheaded, but who is this about whom I hear such things?" And he sought to see him.

Jesus Feeds the Five Thousand

¹⁰ On their return the apostles told him all that they had done. And he took them and withdrew apart to a town called Beth-

saida. [11] When the crowds learned it, they followed him, and he welcomed them and spoke to them of the kingdom of God and cured those who had need of healing. [12] Now the day began to wear away, and the twelve came and said to him, "Send the crowd away to go into the surrounding villages and countryside to find lodging and get provisions, for we are here in a desolate place." [13] But he said to them, "You give them something to eat." They said, "We have no more than five loaves and two fish—unless we are to go and buy food for all these people." [14] For there were about five thousand men. And he said to his disciples, "Have them sit down in groups of about fifty each." [15] And they did so, and had them all sit down. [16] And taking the five loaves and the two fish, he looked up to heaven and said a blessing over them. Then he broke the loaves and gave them to the disciples to set before the crowd. [17] And they all ate and were satisfied. And what was left over was picked up, twelve baskets of broken pieces.

Peter Confesses Jesus as the Christ

[18] Now it happened that as he was praying alone, the disciples were with him. And he asked them, "Who do the crowds say that I am?" [19] And they answered, "John the Baptist. But others say, Elijah, and others, that one of the prophets of old has risen." [20] Then he said to them, "But who do you say that I am?" And Peter answered, "The Christ of God."

Jesus Foretells His Death

[21] And he strictly charged and commanded them to tell this to no one, [22] saying, "The Son of Man must suffer many things and be rejected by the elders and chief priests and scribes, and be killed, and on the third day be raised."

Take Up Your Cross and Follow Jesus

²³ And he said to all, "If anyone would come after me, let him deny himself and take up his cross daily and follow me. ²⁴ For whoever would save his life will lose it, but whoever loses his life for my sake will save it. ²⁵ For what does it profit a man if he gains the whole world and loses or forfeits himself? ²⁶ For whoever is ashamed of me and of my words, of him will the Son of Man be ashamed when he comes in his glory and the glory of the Father and of the holy angels. ²⁷ But I tell you truly, there are some standing here who will not taste death until they see the kingdom of God."

The Transfiguration

²⁸ Now about eight days after these sayings he took with him Peter and John and James and went up on the mountain to pray. ²⁹ And as he was praying, the appearance of his face was altered, and his clothing became dazzling white. ³⁰ And behold, two men were talking with him, Moses and Elijah, ³¹ who appeared in glory and spoke of his departure, which he was about to accomplish at Jerusalem. ³² Now Peter and those who were with him were heavy with sleep, but when they became fully awake they saw his glory and the two men who stood with him. ³³ And as the men were parting from him, Peter said to Jesus, "Master, it is good that we are here. Let us make three tents, one for you and one for Moses and one for Elijah"—not knowing what he said. ³⁴ As he was saying these things, a cloud came and overshadowed them, and they were afraid as they entered the cloud. ³⁵ And a voice came out of the cloud, saying, "This is my Son, my Chosen One; listen to him!" ³⁶ And when the voice had spoken, Jesus was found alone. And they kept silent and told no one in those days anything of what they had seen.

Jesus Heals a Boy with an Unclean Spirit

³⁷ On the next day, when they had come down from the mountain, a great crowd met him. ³⁸ And behold, a man from the crowd cried out, "Teacher, I beg you to look at my son, for he is my only child. ³⁹ And behold, a spirit seizes him, and he suddenly cries out. It convulses him so that he foams at the mouth, and shatters him, and will hardly leave him. ⁴⁰ And I begged your disciples to cast it out, but they could not." ⁴¹ Jesus answered, "O faithless and twisted generation, how long am I to be with you and bear with you? Bring your son here." ⁴² While he was coming, the demon threw him to the ground and convulsed him. But Jesus rebuked the unclean spirit and healed the boy, and gave him back to his father. ⁴³ And all were astonished at the majesty of God.

Jesus Again Foretells His Death

But while they were all marveling at everything he was doing, Jesus said to his disciples, ⁴⁴ "Let these words sink into your ears: The Son of Man is about to be delivered into the hands of men." ⁴⁵ But they did not understand this saying, and it was concealed from them, so that they might not perceive it. And they were afraid to ask him about this saying.

Who Is the Greatest?

⁴⁶ An argument arose among them as to which of them was the greatest. ⁴⁷ But Jesus, knowing the reasoning of their hearts, took a child and put him by his side ⁴⁸ and said to them, "Whoever receives this child in my name receives me, and whoever receives me receives him who sent me. For he who is least among you all is the one who is great."

Anyone Not Against Us Is For Us

⁴⁹ John answered, "Master, we saw someone casting out demons in your name, and we tried to stop him, because he

does not follow with us." ⁵⁰ But Jesus said to him, "Do not stop him, for the one who is not against you is for you."

A Samaritan Village Rejects Jesus

⁵¹ When the days drew near for him to be taken up, he set his face to go to Jerusalem. ⁵² And he sent messengers ahead of him, who went and entered a village of the Samaritans, to make preparations for him. ⁵³ But the people did not receive him, because his face was set toward Jerusalem. ⁵⁴ And when his disciples James and John saw it, they said, "Lord, do you want us to tell fire to come down from heaven and consume them?" ⁵⁵ But he turned and rebuked them. ⁵⁶ And they went on to another village.

The Cost of Following Jesus

⁵⁷ As they were going along the road, someone said to him, "I will follow you wherever you go." ⁵⁸ And Jesus said to him, "Foxes have holes, and birds of the air have nests, but the Son of Man has nowhere to lay his head." ⁵⁹ To another he said, "Follow me." But he said, "Lord, let me first go and bury my father." ⁶⁰ And Jesus said to him, "Leave the dead to bury their own dead. But as for you, go and proclaim the kingdom of God." ⁶¹ Yet another said, "I will follow you, Lord, but let me first say farewell to those at my home." ⁶² Jesus said to him, "No one who puts his hand to the plow and looks back is fit for the kingdom of God."

Jesus Sends Out the Seventy-Two

10 After this the Lord appointed seventy-two others and sent them on ahead of him, two by two, into every town and place where he himself was about to go. ² And he said to them, "The harvest is plentiful, but the laborers are few. Therefore pray earnestly to the Lord of the harvest to send out laborers into his harvest. ³ Go your way; behold, I am sending you out as lambs in the midst of wolves. ⁴ Carry no moneybag, no knapsack, no sandals, and greet no one on the road. ⁵ Whatever house you enter, first say, 'Peace be to this house!' ⁶ And if a son of peace is there, your peace will rest upon him. But if not, it will return to you. ⁷ And remain in the same house, eating and drinking what they provide, for the laborer deserves his wages. Do not go from house to house. ⁸ Whenever you enter a town and they receive you, eat what is set before you. ⁹ Heal the sick in it and say to them, 'The kingdom of God has come near to you.' ¹⁰ But whenever you enter a town and they do not receive you, go into its streets and say, ¹¹ 'Even the dust of your town that clings to our feet we wipe off against you. Nevertheless know this, that the kingdom of God has come near.' ¹² I tell you, it will be more bearable on that day for Sodom than for that town.

Woe to Unrepentant Cities

¹³ "Woe to you, Chorazin! Woe to you, Bethsaida! For if the mighty works done in you had been done in Tyre and Sidon, they would have repented long ago, sitting in sackcloth and ashes. ¹⁴ But it will be more bearable in the judgment for Tyre and Sidon than for you. ¹⁵ And you, Capernaum, will you be exalted to heaven? You shall be brought down to Hades.

¹⁶ "The one who hears you hears me, and the one who rejects you rejects me, and the one who rejects me rejects him who sent me."

The Return of the Seventy-Two

¹⁷ The seventy-two returned with joy, saying, "Lord, even the demons are subject to us in your name!" ¹⁸ And he said to them, "I saw Satan fall like lightning from heaven. ¹⁹ Behold, I have

given you authority to tread on serpents and scorpions, and over all the power of the enemy, and nothing shall hurt you. ²⁰ Nevertheless, do not rejoice in this, that the spirits are subject to you, but rejoice that your names are written in heaven."

Jesus Rejoices in the Father's Will

²¹ In that same hour he rejoiced in the Holy Spirit and said, "I thank you, Father, Lord of heaven and earth, that you have hidden these things from the wise and understanding and revealed them to little children; yes, Father, for such was your gracious will. ²² All things have been handed over to me by my Father, and no one knows who the Son is except the Father, or who the Father is except the Son and anyone to whom the Son chooses to reveal him."

²³ Then turning to the disciples he said privately, "Blessed are the eyes that see what you see! ²⁴ For I tell you that many prophets and kings desired to see what you see, and did not see it, and to hear what you hear, and did not hear it."

The Parable of the Good Samaritan

²⁵ And behold, a lawyer stood up to put him to the test, saying, "Teacher, what shall I do to inherit eternal life?" ²⁶ He said to him, "What is written in the Law? How do you read it?" ²⁷ And he answered, "You shall love the Lord your God with all your heart and with all your soul and with all your strength and with all your mind, and your neighbor as yourself." ²⁸ And he said to him, "You have answered correctly; do this, and you will live."

²⁹ But he, desiring to justify himself, said to Jesus, "And who is my neighbor?" ³⁰ Jesus replied, "A man was going down from Jerusalem to Jericho, and he fell among robbers, who stripped him and beat him and departed, leaving him half dead. ³¹ Now by chance a priest was going down that road, and when he saw him he passed by on the other side. ³² So likewise a Levite, when

he came to the place and saw him, passed by on the other side. ³³ But a Samaritan, as he journeyed, came to where he was, and when he saw him, he had compassion. ³⁴ He went to him and bound up his wounds, pouring on oil and wine. Then he set him on his own animal and brought him to an inn and took care of him. ³⁵ And the next day he took out two denarii and gave them to the innkeeper, saying, 'Take care of him, and whatever more you spend, I will repay you when I come back.' ³⁶ Which of these three, do you think, proved to be a neighbor to the man who fell among the robbers?" ³⁷ He said, "The one who showed him mercy." And Jesus said to him, "You go, and do likewise."

Martha and Mary

³⁸ Now as they went on their way, Jesus entered a village. And a woman named Martha welcomed him into her house. ³⁹ And she had a sister called Mary, who sat at the Lord's feet and listened to his teaching. ⁴⁰ But Martha was distracted with much serving. And she went up to him and said, "Lord, do you not care that my sister has left me to serve alone? Tell her then to help me." ⁴¹ But the Lord answered her, "Martha, Martha, you are anxious and troubled about many things, ⁴² but one thing is necessary. Mary has chosen the good portion, which will not be taken away from her."

The Lord's Prayer

11 Now Jesus was praying in a certain place, and when he finished, one of his disciples said to him, "Lord, teach us to pray, as John taught his disciples." ² And he said to them, "When you pray, say:

> "Father, hallowed be your name.
>   Your kingdom come.
>   ³ Give us each day our daily bread,

> [4] and forgive us our sins,
>> for we ourselves forgive
>> everyone who is indebted to us.
> And lead us not into temptation."

[5] And he said to them, "Which of you who has a friend will go to him at midnight and say to him, 'Friend, lend me three loaves, [6] for a friend of mine has arrived on a journey, and I have nothing to set before him'; [7] and he will answer from within, 'Do not bother me; the door is now shut, and my children are with me in bed. I cannot get up and give you anything'? [8] I tell you, though he will not get up and give him anything because he is his friend, yet because of his impudence he will rise and give him whatever he needs. [9] And I tell you, ask, and it will be given to you; seek, and you will find; knock, and it will be opened to you. [10] For everyone who asks receives, and the one who seeks finds, and to the one who knocks it will be opened. [11] What father among you, if his son asks for a fish, will instead of a fish give him a serpent; [12] or if he asks for an egg, will give him a scorpion? [13] If you then, who are evil, know how to give good gifts to your children, how much more will the heavenly Father give the Holy Spirit to those who ask him!"

Jesus and Beelzebul

[14] Now he was casting out a demon that was mute. When the demon had gone out, the mute man spoke, and the people marveled. [15] But some of them said, "He casts out demons by Beelzebul, the prince of demons," [16] while others, to test him, kept seeking from him a sign from heaven. [17] But he, knowing their thoughts, said to them, "Every kingdom divided against itself is laid waste, and a divided household falls. [18] And if Satan also is divided against himself, how will his kingdom stand? For you say that I cast out demons by Beelzebul. [19] And if I cast out

demons by Beelzebul, by whom do your sons cast them out? Therefore they will be your judges. ²⁰ But if it is by the finger of God that I cast out demons, then the kingdom of God has come upon you. ²¹ When a strong man, fully armed, guards his own palace, his goods are safe; ²² but when one stronger than he attacks him and overcomes him, he takes away his armor in which he trusted and divides his spoil. ²³ Whoever is not with me is against me, and whoever does not gather with me scatters.

Return of an Unclean Spirit

²⁴ "When the unclean spirit has gone out of a person, it passes through waterless places seeking rest, and finding none it says, 'I will return to my house from which I came.' ²⁵ And when it comes, it finds the house swept and put in order. ²⁶ Then it goes and brings seven other spirits more evil than itself, and they enter and dwell there. And the last state of that person is worse than the first."

True Blessedness

²⁷ As he said these things, a woman in the crowd raised her voice and said to him, "Blessed is the womb that bore you, and the breasts at which you nursed!" ²⁸ But he said, "Blessed rather are those who hear the word of God and keep it!"

The Sign of Jonah

²⁹ When the crowds were increasing, he began to say, "This generation is an evil generation. It seeks for a sign, but no sign will be given to it except the sign of Jonah. ³⁰ For as Jonah became a sign to the people of Nineveh, so will the Son of Man be to this generation. ³¹ The queen of the South will rise up at the judgment with the men of this generation and condemn them, for she came from the ends of the earth to hear the wisdom of Solomon, and behold, something greater than Solomon is here. ³² The men of Nineveh will rise up at the judgment with this

generation and condemn it, for they repented at the preaching of Jonah, and behold, something greater than Jonah is here.

The Light in You

[33] "No one after lighting a lamp puts it in a cellar or under a basket, but on a stand, so that those who enter may see the light. [34] Your eye is the lamp of your body. When your eye is healthy, your whole body is full of light, but when it is bad, your body is full of darkness. [35] Therefore be careful lest the light in you be darkness. [36] If then your whole body is full of light, having no part dark, it will be wholly bright, as when a lamp with its rays gives you light."

Woes to the Pharisees and Lawyers

[37] While Jesus was speaking, a Pharisee asked him to dine with him, so he went in and reclined at table. [38] The Pharisee was astonished to see that he did not first wash before dinner. [39] And the Lord said to him, "Now you Pharisees cleanse the outside of the cup and of the dish, but inside you are full of greed and wickedness. [40] You fools! Did not he who made the outside make the inside also? [41] But give as alms those things that are within, and behold, everything is clean for you.

[42] "But woe to you Pharisees! For you tithe mint and rue and every herb, and neglect justice and the love of God. These you ought to have done, without neglecting the others. [43] Woe to you Pharisees! For you love the best seat in the synagogues and greetings in the marketplaces. [44] Woe to you! For you are like unmarked graves, and people walk over them without knowing it."

[45] One of the lawyers answered him, "Teacher, in saying these things you insult us also." [46] And he said, "Woe to you lawyers also! For you load people with burdens hard to bear, and you yourselves do not touch the burdens with one of your fingers.

⁴⁷ Woe to you! For you build the tombs of the prophets whom your fathers killed. ⁴⁸ So you are witnesses and you consent to the deeds of your fathers, for they killed them, and you build their tombs. ⁴⁹ Therefore also the Wisdom of God said, 'I will send them prophets and apostles, some of whom they will kill and persecute,' ⁵⁰ so that the blood of all the prophets, shed from the foundation of the world, may be charged against this generation, ⁵¹ from the blood of Abel to the blood of Zechariah, who perished between the altar and the sanctuary. Yes, I tell you, it will be required of this generation. ⁵² Woe to you lawyers! For you have taken away the key of knowledge. You did not enter yourselves, and you hindered those who were entering."

⁵³ As he went away from there, the scribes and the Pharisees began to press him hard and to provoke him to speak about many things, ⁵⁴ lying in wait for him, to catch him in something he might say.

Beware of the Leaven of the Pharisees

12 In the meantime, when so many thousands of the people had gathered together that they were trampling one another, he began to say to his disciples first, "Beware of the leaven of the Pharisees, which is hypocrisy. ² Nothing is covered up that will not be revealed, or hidden that will not be known. ³ Therefore whatever you have said in the dark shall be heard in the light, and what you have whispered in private rooms shall be proclaimed on the housetops.

Have No Fear

⁴ "I tell you, my friends, do not fear those who kill the body, and after that have nothing more that they can do. ⁵ But I will warn you whom to fear: fear him who, after he has killed, has authority to cast into hell. Yes, I tell you, fear him! ⁶ Are not

five sparrows sold for two pennies? And not one of them is for-gotten before God. [7] Why, even the hairs of your head are all numbered. Fear not; you are of more value than many sparrows.

Acknowledge Christ Before Men

[8] "And I tell you, everyone who acknowledges me before men, the Son of Man also will acknowledge before the angels of God, [9] but the one who denies me before men will be denied before the angels of God. [10] And everyone who speaks a word against the Son of Man will be forgiven, but the one who blasphemes against the Holy Spirit will not be forgiven. [11] And when they bring you before the synagogues and the rulers and the authori-ties, do not be anxious about how you should defend yourself or what you should say, [12] for the Holy Spirit will teach you in that very hour what you ought to say."

The Parable of the Rich Fool

[13] Someone in the crowd said to him, "Teacher, tell my brother to divide the inheritance with me." [14] But he said to him, "Man, who made me a judge or arbitrator over you?" [15] And he said to them, "Take care, and be on your guard against all covetousness, for one's life does not consist in the abundance of his possessions." [16] And he told them a parable, saying, "The land of a rich man produced plentifully, [17] and he thought to himself, 'What shall I do, for I have nowhere to store my crops?' [18] And he said, 'I will do this: I will tear down my barns and build larger ones, and there I will store all my grain and my goods. [19] And I will say to my soul, "Soul, you have ample goods laid up for many years; relax, eat, drink, be merry."' [20] But God said to him, 'Fool! This night your soul is required of you, and the things you have prepared, whose will they be?' [21] So is the one who lays up treasure for himself and is not rich toward God."

Do Not Be Anxious

²² And he said to his disciples, "Therefore I tell you, do not be anxious about your life, what you will eat, nor about your body, what you will put on. ²³ For life is more than food, and the body more than clothing. ²⁴ Consider the ravens: they neither sow nor reap, they have neither storehouse nor barn, and yet God feeds them. Of how much more value are you than the birds! ²⁵ And which of you by being anxious can add a single hour to his span of life? ²⁶ If then you are not able to do as small a thing as that, why are you anxious about the rest? ²⁷ Consider the lilies, how they grow: they neither toil nor spin, yet I tell you, even Solomon in all his glory was not arrayed like one of these. ²⁸ But if God so clothes the grass, which is alive in the field today, and tomorrow is thrown into the oven, how much more will he clothe you, O you of little faith! ²⁹ And do not seek what you are to eat and what you are to drink, nor be worried. ³⁰ For all the nations of the world seek after these things, and your Father knows that you need them. ³¹ Instead, seek his kingdom, and these things will be added to you.

³² "Fear not, little flock, for it is your Father's good pleasure to give you the kingdom. ³³ Sell your possessions, and give to the needy. Provide yourselves with moneybags that do not grow old, with a treasure in the heavens that does not fail, where no thief approaches and no moth destroys. ³⁴ For where your treasure is, there will your heart be also.

You Must Be Ready

³⁵ "Stay dressed for action and keep your lamps burning, ³⁶ and be like men who are waiting for their master to come home from the wedding feast, so that they may open the door to him at once when he comes and knocks. ³⁷ Blessed are those servants whom the master finds awake when he comes. Truly, I say to you, he will dress himself for service and have them recline at table, and he will come and serve them. ³⁸ If he comes in the second watch,

or in the third, and finds them awake, blessed are those servants! ³⁹ But know this, that if the master of the house had known at what hour the thief was coming, he would not have left his house to be broken into. ⁴⁰ You also must be ready, for the Son of Man is coming at an hour you do not expect."

⁴¹ Peter said, "Lord, are you telling this parable for us or for all?" ⁴² And the Lord said, "Who then is the faithful and wise manager, whom his master will set over his household, to give them their portion of food at the proper time? ⁴³ Blessed is that servant whom his master will find so doing when he comes. ⁴⁴ Truly, I say to you, he will set him over all his possessions. ⁴⁵ But if that servant says to himself, 'My master is delayed in coming,' and begins to beat the male and female servants, and to eat and drink and get drunk, ⁴⁶ the master of that servant will come on a day when he does not expect him and at an hour he does not know, and will cut him in pieces and put him with the unfaithful. ⁴⁷ And that servant who knew his master's will but did not get ready or act according to his will, will receive a severe beating. ⁴⁸ But the one who did not know, and did what deserved a beating, will receive a light beating. Everyone to whom much was given, of him much will be required, and from him to whom they entrusted much, they will demand the more.

Not Peace, but Division

⁴⁹ "I came to cast fire on the earth, and would that it were already kindled! ⁵⁰ I have a baptism to be baptized with, and how great is my distress until it is accomplished! ⁵¹ Do you think that I have come to give peace on earth? No, I tell you, but rather division. ⁵² For from now on in one house there will be five divided, three against two and two against three. ⁵³ They will be divided, father against son and son against father, mother against daughter and daughter against mother, mother-in-law against her daughter-in-law and daughter-in-law against mother-in-law."

Interpreting the Time

⁵⁴ He also said to the crowds, "When you see a cloud rising in the west, you say at once, 'A shower is coming.' And so it happens. ⁵⁵ And when you see the south wind blowing, you say, 'There will be scorching heat,' and it happens. ⁵⁶ You hypocrites! You know how to interpret the appearance of earth and sky, but why do you not know how to interpret the present time?

Settle with Your Accuser

⁵⁷ "And why do you not judge for yourselves what is right? ⁵⁸ As you go with your accuser before the magistrate, make an effort to settle with him on the way, lest he drag you to the judge, and the judge hand you over to the officer, and the officer put you in prison. ⁵⁹ I tell you, you will never get out until you have paid the very last penny."

Repent or Perish

13 There were some present at that very time who told him about the Galileans whose blood Pilate had mingled with their sacrifices. ² And he answered them, "Do you think that these Galileans were worse sinners than all the other Galileans, because they suffered in this way? ³ No, I tell you; but unless you repent, you will all likewise perish. ⁴ Or those eighteen on whom the tower in Siloam fell and killed them: do you think that they were worse offenders than all the others who lived in Jerusalem? ⁵ No, I tell you; but unless you repent, you will all likewise perish."

The Parable of the Barren Fig Tree

⁶ And he told this parable: "A man had a fig tree planted in his vineyard, and he came seeking fruit on it and found none. ⁷ And he said to the vinedresser, 'Look, for three years now I have come seeking fruit on this fig tree, and I find none. Cut

it down. Why should it use up the ground?' ⁸ And he answered him, 'Sir, let it alone this year also, until I dig around it and put on manure. ⁹ Then if it should bear fruit next year, well and good; but if not, you can cut it down.'"

A Woman with a Disabling Spirit

¹⁰ Now he was teaching in one of the synagogues on the Sabbath. ¹¹ And behold, there was a woman who had had a disabling spirit for eighteen years. She was bent over and could not fully straighten herself. ¹² When Jesus saw her, he called her over and said to her, "Woman, you are freed from your disability." ¹³ And he laid his hands on her, and immediately she was made straight, and she glorified God. ¹⁴ But the ruler of the synagogue, indignant because Jesus had healed on the Sabbath, said to the people, "There are six days in which work ought to be done. Come on those days and be healed, and not on the Sabbath day." ¹⁵ Then the Lord answered him, "You hypocrites! Does not each of you on the Sabbath untie his ox or his donkey from the manger and lead it away to water it? ¹⁶ And ought not this woman, a daughter of Abraham whom Satan bound for eighteen years, be loosed from this bond on the Sabbath day?" ¹⁷ As he said these things, all his adversaries were put to shame, and all the people rejoiced at all the glorious things that were done by him.

The Mustard Seed and the Leaven

¹⁸ He said therefore, "What is the kingdom of God like? And to what shall I compare it? ¹⁹ It is like a grain of mustard seed that a man took and sowed in his garden, and it grew and became a tree, and the birds of the air made nests in its branches."

²⁰ And again he said, "To what shall I compare the kingdom of God? ²¹ It is like leaven that a woman took and hid in three measures of flour, until it was all leavened."

The Narrow Door

²² He went on his way through towns and villages, teaching and journeying toward Jerusalem. ²³ And someone said to him, "Lord, will those who are saved be few?" And he said to them, ²⁴ "Strive to enter through the narrow door. For many, I tell you, will seek to enter and will not be able. ²⁵ When once the master of the house has risen and shut the door, and you begin to stand outside and to knock at the door, saying, 'Lord, open to us,' then he will answer you, 'I do not know where you come from.' ²⁶ Then you will begin to say, 'We ate and drank in your presence, and you taught in our streets.' ²⁷ But he will say, 'I tell you, I do not know where you come from. Depart from me, all you workers of evil!' ²⁸ In that place there will be weeping and gnashing of teeth, when you see Abraham and Isaac and Jacob and all the prophets in the kingdom of God but you yourselves cast out. ²⁹ And people will come from east and west, and from north and south, and recline at table in the kingdom of God. ³⁰ And behold, some are last who will be first, and some are first who will be last."

Lament over Jerusalem

³¹ At that very hour some Pharisees came and said to him, "Get away from here, for Herod wants to kill you." ³² And he said to them, "Go and tell that fox, 'Behold, I cast out demons and perform cures today and tomorrow, and the third day I finish my course. ³³ Nevertheless, I must go on my way today and tomorrow and the day following, for it cannot be that a prophet should perish away from Jerusalem.' ³⁴ O Jerusalem, Jerusalem, the city that kills the prophets and stones those who are sent to it! How often would I have gathered your children together as a hen gathers her brood under her wings, and you were not willing! ³⁵ Behold, your house is forsaken. And I tell

you, you will not see me until you say, 'Blessed is he who comes in the name of the Lord!'"

Healing of a Man on the Sabbath

14 One Sabbath, when he went to dine at the house of a ruler of the Pharisees, they were watching him carefully. ² And behold, there was a man before him who had dropsy. ³ And Jesus responded to the lawyers and Pharisees, saying, "Is it lawful to heal on the Sabbath, or not?" ⁴ But they remained silent. Then he took him and healed him and sent him away. ⁵ And he said to them, "Which of you, having a son or an ox that has fallen into a well on a Sabbath day, will not immediately pull him out?" ⁶ And they could not reply to these things.

The Parable of the Wedding Feast

⁷ Now he told a parable to those who were invited, when he noticed how they chose the places of honor, saying to them, ⁸ "When you are invited by someone to a wedding feast, do not sit down in a place of honor, lest someone more distinguished than you be invited by him, ⁹ and he who invited you both will come and say to you, 'Give your place to this person,' and then you will begin with shame to take the lowest place. ¹⁰ But when you are invited, go and sit in the lowest place, so that when your host comes he may say to you, 'Friend, move up higher.' Then you will be honored in the presence of all who sit at table with you. ¹¹ For everyone who exalts himself will be humbled, and he who humbles himself will be exalted."

The Parable of the Great Banquet

¹² He said also to the man who had invited him, "When you give a dinner or a banquet, do not invite your friends or your brothers or your relatives or rich neighbors, lest they also invite

you in return and you be repaid. [13] But when you give a feast, invite the poor, the crippled, the lame, the blind, [14] and you will be blessed, because they cannot repay you. For you will be repaid at the resurrection of the just."

[15] When one of those who reclined at table with him heard these things, he said to him, "Blessed is everyone who will eat bread in the kingdom of God!" [16] But he said to him, "A man once gave a great banquet and invited many. [17] And at the time for the banquet he sent his servant to say to those who had been invited, 'Come, for everything is now ready.' [18] But they all alike began to make excuses. The first said to him, 'I have bought a field, and I must go out and see it. Please have me excused.' [19] And another said, 'I have bought five yoke of oxen, and I go to examine them. Please have me excused.' [20] And another said, 'I have married a wife, and therefore I cannot come.' [21] So the servant came and reported these things to his master. Then the master of the house became angry and said to his servant, 'Go out quickly to the streets and lanes of the city, and bring in the poor and crippled and blind and lame.' [22] And the servant said, 'Sir, what you commanded has been done, and still there is room.' [23] And the master said to the servant, 'Go out to the highways and hedges and compel people to come in, that my house may be filled. [24] For I tell you, none of those men who were invited shall taste my banquet.'"

The Cost of Discipleship

[25] Now great crowds accompanied him, and he turned and said to them, [26] "If anyone comes to me and does not hate his own father and mother and wife and children and brothers and sisters, yes, and even his own life, he cannot be my disciple. [27] Whoever does not bear his own cross and come after me cannot be my disciple. [28] For which of you, desiring to build a tower, does not first sit down and count the cost, whether

he has enough to complete it? ²⁹ Otherwise, when he has laid a foundation and is not able to finish, all who see it begin to mock him, ³⁰ saying, 'This man began to build and was not able to finish.' ³¹ Or what king, going out to encounter another king in war, will not sit down first and deliberate whether he is able with ten thousand to meet him who comes against him with twenty thousand? ³² And if not, while the other is yet a great way off, he sends a delegation and asks for terms of peace. ³³ So therefore, any one of you who does not renounce all that he has cannot be my disciple.

Salt Without Taste Is Worthless

³⁴ "Salt is good, but if salt has lost its taste, how shall its saltiness be restored? ³⁵ It is of no use either for the soil or for the manure pile. It is thrown away. He who has ears to hear, let him hear."

The Parable of the Lost Sheep

15 Now the tax collectors and sinners were all drawing near to hear him. ² And the Pharisees and the scribes grumbled, saying, "This man receives sinners and eats with them."

³ So he told them this parable: ⁴ "What man of you, having a hundred sheep, if he has lost one of them, does not leave the ninety-nine in the open country, and go after the one that is lost, until he finds it? ⁵ And when he has found it, he lays it on his shoulders, rejoicing. ⁶ And when he comes home, he calls together his friends and his neighbors, saying to them, 'Rejoice with me, for I have found my sheep that was lost.' ⁷ Just so, I tell you, there will be more joy in heaven over one sinner who repents than over ninety-nine righteous persons who need no repentance.

The Parable of the Lost Coin

⁸ "Or what woman, having ten silver coins, if she loses one coin, does not light a lamp and sweep the house and seek diligently until she finds it? ⁹ And when she has found it, she calls together her friends and neighbors, saying, 'Rejoice with me, for I have found the coin that I had lost.' ¹⁰ Just so, I tell you, there is joy before the angels of God over one sinner who repents."

The Parable of the Prodigal Son

¹¹ And he said, "There was a man who had two sons. ¹² And the younger of them said to his father, 'Father, give me the share of property that is coming to me.' And he divided his property between them. ¹³ Not many days later, the younger son gathered all he had and took a journey into a far country, and there he squandered his property in reckless living. ¹⁴ And when he had spent everything, a severe famine arose in that country, and he began to be in need. ¹⁵ So he went and hired himself out to one of the citizens of that country, who sent him into his fields to feed pigs. ¹⁶ And he was longing to be fed with the pods that the pigs ate, and no one gave him anything.

¹⁷ "But when he came to himself, he said, 'How many of my father's hired servants have more than enough bread, but I perish here with hunger! ¹⁸ I will arise and go to my father, and I will say to him, "Father, I have sinned against heaven and before you. ¹⁹ I am no longer worthy to be called your son. Treat me as one of your hired servants."' ²⁰ And he arose and came to his father. But while he was still a long way off, his father saw him and felt compassion, and ran and embraced him and kissed him. ²¹ And the son said to him, 'Father, I have sinned against heaven and before you. I am no longer worthy to be called your son.' ²² But the father said to his servants, 'Bring quickly the best robe, and put it on him, and put a ring on his hand, and shoes on his feet. ²³ And bring the fattened calf and kill it, and let us eat and

celebrate. ²⁴ For this my son was dead, and is alive again; he was lost, and is found.' And they began to celebrate.

²⁵ "Now his older son was in the field, and as he came and drew near to the house, he heard music and dancing. ²⁶ And he called one of the servants and asked what these things meant. ²⁷ And he said to him, 'Your brother has come, and your father has killed the fattened calf, because he has received him back safe and sound.' ²⁸ But he was angry and refused to go in. His father came out and entreated him, ²⁹ but he answered his father, 'Look, these many years I have served you, and I never disobeyed your command, yet you never gave me a young goat, that I might celebrate with my friends. ³⁰ But when this son of yours came, who has devoured your property with prostitutes, you killed the fattened calf for him!' ³¹ And he said to him, 'Son, you are always with me, and all that is mine is yours. ³² It was fitting to celebrate and be glad, for this your brother was dead, and is alive; he was lost, and is found.'"

The Parable of the Dishonest Manager

16 He also said to the disciples, "There was a rich man who had a manager, and charges were brought to him that this man was wasting his possessions. ² And he called him and said to him, 'What is this that I hear about you? Turn in the account of your management, for you can no longer be manager.' ³ And the manager said to himself, 'What shall I do, since my master is taking the management away from me? I am not strong enough to dig, and I am ashamed to beg. ⁴ I have decided what to do, so that when I am removed from management, people may receive me into their houses.' ⁵ So, summoning his master's debtors one by one, he said to the first, 'How much do you owe my master?' ⁶ He said, 'A hundred measures of oil.' He said to him, 'Take your bill, and sit down quickly and write fifty.' ⁷ Then he said to another, 'And how much do you owe?' He said, 'A hundred measures of wheat.' He said to him, 'Take your bill, and write eighty.' ⁸ The master commended the dishonest manager for his shrewdness. For the sons of this world are more shrewd in dealing with their own generation than the sons of light. ⁹ And I tell you, make friends for yourselves by means of unrighteous wealth, so that when it fails they may receive you into the eternal dwellings.

¹⁰ "One who is faithful in a very little is also faithful in much, and one who is dishonest in a very little is also dishonest in much. ¹¹ If then you have not been faithful in the unrighteous wealth, who will entrust to you the true riches? ¹² And if you have not been faithful in that which is another's, who will give you that which is your own? ¹³ No servant can serve two masters, for either he will hate the one and love the other, or he will be devoted to the one and despise the other. You cannot serve God and money."

The Law and the Kingdom of God

¹⁴ The Pharisees, who were lovers of money, heard all these things, and they ridiculed him. ¹⁵ And he said to them, "You are those who justify yourselves before men, but God knows your hearts. For what is exalted among men is an abomination in the sight of God.

¹⁶ "The Law and the Prophets were until John; since then the good news of the kingdom of God is preached, and everyone forces his way into it. ¹⁷ But it is easier for heaven and earth to pass away than for one dot of the Law to become void.

Divorce and Remarriage

¹⁸ "Everyone who divorces his wife and marries another commits adultery, and he who marries a woman divorced from her husband commits adultery.

The Rich Man and Lazarus

[19] "There was a rich man who was clothed in purple and fine linen and who feasted sumptuously every day. [20] And at his gate was laid a poor man named Lazarus, covered with sores, [21] who desired to be fed with what fell from the rich man's table. Moreover, even the dogs came and licked his sores. [22] The poor man died and was carried by the angels to Abraham's side. The rich man also died and was buried, [23] and in Hades, being in torment, he lifted up his eyes and saw Abraham far off and Lazarus at his side. [24] And he called out, 'Father Abraham, have mercy on me, and send Lazarus to dip the end of his finger in water and cool my tongue, for I am in anguish in this flame.' [25] But Abraham said, 'Child, remember that you in your lifetime received your good things, and Lazarus in like manner bad things; but now he is comforted here, and you are in anguish. [26] And besides all this, between us and you a great chasm has been fixed, in order that those who would pass from here to you may not be able, and none may cross from there to us.' [27] And he said, 'Then I beg you, father, to send him to my father's house— [28] for I have five brothers—so that he may warn them, lest they also come into this place of torment.' [29] But Abraham said, 'They have Moses and the Prophets; let them hear them.' [30] And he said, 'No, father Abraham, but if someone goes to them from the dead, they will repent.' [31] He said to him, 'If they do not hear Moses and the Prophets, neither will they be convinced if someone should rise from the dead.'"

Temptations to Sin

17 And he said to his disciples, "Temptations to sin are sure to come, but woe to the one through whom they come! [2] It would be better for him if a millstone were hung around his neck and he were cast into the sea than that he should cause one of these little ones to sin. [3] Pay attention to yourselves! If your brother sins, rebuke him, and if he repents, forgive him, [4] and if he sins against you seven times in the day, and turns to you seven times, saying, 'I repent,' you must forgive him."

Increase Our Faith

[5] The apostles said to the Lord, "Increase our faith!" [6] And the Lord said, "If you had faith like a grain of mustard seed, you could say to this mulberry tree, 'Be uprooted and planted in the sea,' and it would obey you.

Unworthy Servants

[7] "Will any one of you who has a servant plowing or keeping sheep say to him when he has come in from the field, 'Come at once and recline at table'? [8] Will he not rather say to him, 'Prepare supper for me, and dress properly, and serve me while I eat and drink, and afterward you will eat and drink'? [9] Does he thank the servant because he did what was commanded? [10] So you also, when you have done all that you were commanded, say, 'We are unworthy servants; we have only done what was our duty.'"

Jesus Cleanses Ten Lepers

[11] On the way to Jerusalem he was passing along between Samaria and Galilee. [12] And as he entered a village, he was met by ten lepers, who stood at a distance [13] and lifted up their voices, saying, "Jesus, Master, have mercy on us." [14] When he saw them he said to them, "Go and show yourselves to the priests." And as they went they were cleansed. [15] Then one of them, when he saw that he was healed, turned back, praising God with a loud voice; [16] and he fell on his face at Jesus' feet, giving him thanks. Now he was a Samaritan. [17] Then Jesus answered, "Were not ten cleansed? Where are the nine? [18] Was no one found to return

and give praise to God except this foreigner?" ¹⁹ And he said to him, "Rise and go your way; your faith has made you well."

The Coming of the Kingdom

²⁰ Being asked by the Pharisees when the kingdom of God would come, he answered them, "The kingdom of God is not coming in ways that can be observed, ²¹ nor will they say, 'Look, here it is!' or 'There!' for behold, the kingdom of God is in the midst of you."

²² And he said to the disciples, "The days are coming when you will desire to see one of the days of the Son of Man, and you will not see it. ²³ And they will say to you, 'Look, there!' or 'Look, here!' Do not go out or follow them. ²⁴ For as the lightning flashes and lights up the sky from one side to the other, so will the Son of Man be in his day. ²⁵ But first he must suffer many things and be rejected by this generation. ²⁶ Just as it was in the days of Noah, so will it be in the days of the Son of Man. ²⁷ They were eating and drinking and marrying and being given in marriage, until the day when Noah entered the ark, and the flood came and destroyed them all. ²⁸ Likewise, just as it was in the days of Lot—they were eating and drinking, buying and selling, planting and building, ²⁹ but on the day when Lot went out from Sodom, fire and sulfur rained from heaven and destroyed them all— ³⁰ so will it be on the day when the Son of Man is revealed. ³¹ On that day, let the one who is on the housetop, with his goods in the house, not come down to take them away, and likewise let the one who is in the field not turn back. ³² Remember Lot's wife. ³³ Whoever seeks to preserve his life will lose it, but whoever loses his life will keep it. ³⁴ I tell you, in that night there will be two in one bed. One will be taken and the other left. ³⁵ There will be two women grinding together. One will be taken and the other left." ³⁷ And they said to him,

"Where, Lord?" He said to them, "Where the corpse is, there the vultures will gather."

The Parable of the Persistent Widow

18 And he told them a parable to the effect that they ought always to pray and not lose heart. ² He said, "In a certain city there was a judge who neither feared God nor respected man. ³ And there was a widow in that city who kept coming to him and saying, 'Give me justice against my adversary.' ⁴ For a while he refused, but afterward he said to himself, 'Though I neither fear God nor respect man, ⁵ yet because this widow keeps bothering me, I will give her justice, so that she will not beat me down by her continual coming.'" ⁶ And the Lord said, "Hear what the unrighteous judge says. ⁷ And will not God give justice to his elect, who cry to him day and night? Will he delay long over them? ⁸ I tell you, he will give justice to them speedily. Nevertheless, when the Son of Man comes, will he find faith on earth?"

The Pharisee and the Tax Collector

⁹ He also told this parable to some who trusted in themselves that they were righteous, and treated others with contempt: ¹⁰ "Two men went up into the temple to pray, one a Pharisee and the other a tax collector. ¹¹ The Pharisee, standing by himself, prayed thus: 'God, I thank you that I am not like other men, extortioners, unjust, adulterers, or even like this tax collector. ¹² I fast twice a week; I give tithes of all that I get.' ¹³ But the tax collector, standing far off, would not even lift up his eyes to heaven, but beat his breast, saying, 'God, be merciful to me, a sinner!' ¹⁴ I tell you, this man went down to his house justified, rather than the other. For everyone who exalts himself will be humbled, but the one who humbles himself will be exalted."

Let the Children Come to Me

¹⁵ Now they were bringing even infants to him that he might touch them. And when the disciples saw it, they rebuked them. ¹⁶ But Jesus called them to him, saying, "Let the children come to me, and do not hinder them, for to such belongs the kingdom of God. ¹⁷ Truly, I say to you, whoever does not receive the kingdom of God like a child shall not enter it."

The Rich Ruler

¹⁸ And a ruler asked him, "Good Teacher, what must I do to inherit eternal life?" ¹⁹ And Jesus said to him, "Why do you call me good? No one is good except God alone. ²⁰ You know the commandments: 'Do not commit adultery, Do not murder, Do not steal, Do not bear false witness, Honor your father and mother.'" ²¹ And he said, "All these I have kept from my youth." ²² When Jesus heard this, he said to him, "One thing you still lack. Sell all that you have and distribute to the poor, and you will have treasure in heaven; and come, follow me." ²³ But when he heard these things, he became very sad, for he was extremely rich. ²⁴ Jesus, seeing that he had become sad, said, "How difficult it is for those who have wealth to enter the kingdom of God! ²⁵ For it is easier for a camel to go through the eye of a needle than for a rich person to enter the kingdom of God." ²⁶ Those who heard it said, "Then who can be saved?" ²⁷ But he said, "What is impossible with man is possible with God." ²⁸ And Peter said, "See, we have left our homes and followed you." ²⁹ And he said to them, "Truly, I say to you, there is no one who has left house or wife or brothers or parents or children, for the sake of the kingdom of God, ³⁰ who will not receive many times more in this time, and in the age to come eternal life."

Jesus Foretells His Death a Third Time

 ³¹ And taking the twelve, he said to them, "See, we are going up to Jerusalem, and everything that is written about the Son of Man by the prophets will be accomplished. ³² For he will be delivered over to the Gentiles and will be mocked and shamefully treated and spit upon. ³³ And after flogging him, they will kill him, and on the third day he will rise." ³⁴ But they understood none of these things. This saying was hidden from them, and they did not grasp what was said.

Jesus Heals a Blind Beggar

³⁵ As he drew near to Jericho, a blind man was sitting by the roadside begging. ³⁶ And hearing a crowd going by, he inquired what this meant. ³⁷ They told him, "Jesus of Nazareth is passing by." ³⁸ And he cried out, "Jesus, Son of David, have mercy on me!" ³⁹ And those who were in front rebuked him, telling him to be silent. But he cried out all the more, "Son of David, have mercy on me!" ⁴⁰ And Jesus stopped and commanded him to be brought to him. And when he came near, he asked him, ⁴¹ "What do you want me to do for you?" He said, "Lord, let me recover my sight." ⁴² And Jesus said to him, "Recover your sight; your faith has made you well." ⁴³ And immediately he recovered his sight and followed him, glorifying God. And all the people, when they saw it, gave praise to God.

Jesus and Zacchaeus

19 He entered Jericho and was passing through. ² And behold, there was a man named Zacchaeus. He was a chief tax collector and was rich. ³ And he was seeking to see who Jesus was, but on account of the crowd he could not, because he was small in stature. ⁴ So he ran on ahead and climbed up into a sycamore tree to see him, for he was about to pass that way. ⁵ And when Jesus came to the place, he looked up and said to him, "Zacchaeus, hurry and come down, for I must stay at your house today." ⁶ So he hurried and came down and received him joyfully. ⁷ And when they saw it, they all grumbled, "He has gone in to be the guest of a man who is a sinner." ⁸ And Zacchaeus stood and said to the Lord, "Behold, Lord, the half of my goods I give to the poor. And if I have defrauded anyone of anything, I restore it fourfold." ⁹ And Jesus said to him, "Today salvation has come to this house, since he also is a son of Abraham. ¹⁰ For the Son of Man came to seek and to save the lost."

The Parable of the Ten Minas

¹¹ As they heard these things, he proceeded to tell a parable, because he was near to Jerusalem, and because they supposed that the kingdom of God was to appear immediately. ¹² He said therefore, "A nobleman went into a far country to receive for himself a kingdom and then return. ¹³ Calling ten of his servants, he gave them ten minas, and said to them, 'Engage in business until I come.' ¹⁴ But his citizens hated him and sent a delegation after him, saying, 'We do not want this man to reign over us.' ¹⁵ When he returned, having received the kingdom, he ordered these servants to whom he had given the money to be called to him, that he might know what they had gained by doing business. ¹⁶ The first came before him, saying, 'Lord, your mina has made ten minas more.' ¹⁷ And he said to him, 'Well done, good servant! Because you have been faithful in a very little, you shall have authority over ten cities.' ¹⁸ And the second came, saying, 'Lord, your mina has made five minas.' ¹⁹ And he said to him, 'And you are to be over five cities.' ²⁰ Then another came, saying, 'Lord, here is your mina, which I kept laid away in a handkerchief; ²¹ for I was afraid of you, because you are a severe man. You take what you did not deposit, and reap what you did not sow.' ²² He said to him, 'I will condemn you with

your own words, you wicked servant! You knew that I was a severe man, taking what I did not deposit and reaping what I did not sow? ²³ Why then did you not put my money in the bank, and at my coming I might have collected it with interest?' ²⁴ And he said to those who stood by, 'Take the mina from him, and give it to the one who has the ten minas.' ²⁵ And they said to him, 'Lord, he has ten minas!' ²⁶ 'I tell you that to everyone who has, more will be given, but from the one who has not, even what he has will be taken away. ²⁷ But as for these enemies of mine, who did not want me to reign over them, bring them here and slaughter them before me.'"

The Triumphal Entry

²⁸ And when he had said these things, he went on ahead, going up to Jerusalem. ²⁹ When he drew near to Bethphage and Bethany, at the mount that is called Olivet, he sent two of the disciples, ³⁰ saying, "Go into the village in front of you, where on entering you will find a colt tied, on which no one has ever yet sat. Untie it and bring it here. ³¹ If anyone asks you, 'Why are you untying it?' you shall say this: 'The Lord has need of it.'" ³² So those who were sent went away and found it just as he had told them. ³³ And as they were untying the colt, its owners said to them, "Why are you untying the colt?" ³⁴ And they said, "The Lord has need of it." ³⁵ And they brought it to Jesus, and throwing their cloaks on the colt, they set Jesus on it. ³⁶ And as he rode along, they spread their cloaks on the road. ³⁷ As he was drawing near—already on the way down the Mount of Olives—the whole multitude of his disciples began to rejoice and praise God with a loud voice for all the mighty works that they had seen, ³⁸ saying, "Blessed is the King who comes in the name of the Lord! Peace in heaven and glory in the highest!" ³⁹ And some of the Pharisees in the crowd said to him, "Teacher,

rebuke your disciples." [40] He answered, "I tell you, if these were silent, the very stones would cry out."

Jesus Weeps over Jerusalem

[41] And when he drew near and saw the city, he wept over it, [42] saying, "Would that you, even you, had known on this day the things that make for peace! But now they are hidden from your eyes. [43] For the days will come upon you, when your enemies will set up a barricade around you and surround you and hem you in on every side [44] and tear you down to the ground, you and your children within you. And they will not leave one stone upon another in you, because you did not know the time of your visitation."

Jesus Cleanses the Temple

[45] And he entered the temple and began to drive out those who sold, [46] saying to them, "It is written, 'My house shall be a house of prayer,' but you have made it a den of robbers."

[47] And he was teaching daily in the temple. The chief priests and the scribes and the principal men of the people were seeking to destroy him, [48] but they did not find anything they could do, for all the people were hanging on his words.

The Authority of Jesus Challenged

20 One day, as Jesus was teaching the people in the temple and preaching the gospel, the chief priests and the scribes with the elders came up [2] and said to him, "Tell us by what authority you do these things, or who it is that gave you this authority." [3] He answered them, "I also will ask you a question. Now tell me, [4] was the baptism of John from heaven or from man?" [5] And they discussed it with one another, saying, "If we say, 'From heaven,' he will say, 'Why did you not believe him?' [6] But if we say, 'From man,' all the people will stone us to death, for they are convinced that John was a prophet." ⁷ So they answered that they did not know where it came from. ⁸ And Jesus said to them, "Neither will I tell you by what authority I do these things."

The Parable of the Wicked Tenants

⁹ And he began to tell the people this parable: "A man planted a vineyard and let it out to tenants and went into another country for a long while. ¹⁰ When the time came, he sent a servant to the tenants, so that they would give him some of the fruit of the vineyard. But the tenants beat him and sent him away empty-handed. ¹¹ And he sent another servant. But they also beat and treated him shamefully, and sent him away empty-handed. ¹² And he sent yet a third. This one also they wounded and cast out. ¹³ Then the owner of the vineyard said, 'What shall I do? I will send my beloved son; perhaps they will respect him.' ¹⁴ But when the tenants saw him, they said to themselves, 'This is the heir. Let us kill him, so that the inheritance may be ours.' ¹⁵ And they threw him out of the vineyard and killed him. What then will the owner of the vineyard do to them? ¹⁶ He will come and destroy those tenants and give the vineyard to others." When they heard this, they said, "Surely not!" ¹⁷ But he looked directly at them and said, "What then is this that is written:

"'The stone that the builders rejected
　　has become the cornerstone'?

¹⁸ Everyone who falls on that stone will be broken to pieces, and when it falls on anyone, it will crush him."

Paying Taxes to Caesar

¹⁹ The scribes and the chief priests sought to lay hands on him at that very hour, for they perceived that he had told this parable against them, but they feared the people. ²⁰ So they watched

him and sent spies, who pretended to be sincere, that they might catch him in something he said, so as to deliver him up to the authority and jurisdiction of the governor. ²¹ So they asked him, "Teacher, we know that you speak and teach rightly, and show no partiality, but truly teach the way of God. ²² Is it lawful for us to give tribute to Caesar, or not?" ²³ But he perceived their craftiness, and said to them, ²⁴ "Show me a denarius. Whose likeness and inscription does it have?" They said, "Caesar's." ²⁵ He said to them, "Then render to Caesar the things that are Caesar's, and to God the things that are God's." ²⁶ And they were not able in the presence of the people to catch him in what he said, but marveling at his answer they became silent.

Sadducees Ask About the Resurrection

²⁷ There came to him some Sadducees, those who deny that there is a resurrection, ²⁸ and they asked him a question, saying, "Teacher, Moses wrote for us that if a man's brother dies, having a wife but no children, the man must take the widow and raise up offspring for his brother. ²⁹ Now there were seven brothers. The first took a wife, and died without children. ³⁰ And the second ³¹ and the third took her, and likewise all seven left no children and died. ³² Afterward the woman also died. ³³ In the resurrection, therefore, whose wife will the woman be? For the seven had her as wife."

³⁴ And Jesus said to them, "The sons of this age marry and are given in marriage, ³⁵ but those who are considered worthy to attain to that age and to the resurrection from the dead neither marry nor are given in marriage, ³⁶ for they cannot die anymore, because they are equal to angels and are sons of God, being sons of the resurrection. ³⁷ But that the dead are raised, even Moses showed, in the passage about the bush, where he calls the Lord the God of Abraham and the God of Isaac and the God of Jacob. ³⁸ Now he is not God of the dead, but of the living, for all live to

him." [39] Then some of the scribes answered, "Teacher, you have spoken well." [40] For they no longer dared to ask him any question.

Whose Son Is the Christ?

[41] But he said to them, "How can they say that the Christ is David's son? [42] For David himself says in the Book of Psalms,

> "'The Lord said to my Lord,
>> "Sit at my right hand,
>>> [43] until I make your enemies your footstool."'

[44] David thus calls him Lord, so how is he his son?"

Beware of the Scribes

[45] And in the hearing of all the people he said to his disciples, [46] "Beware of the scribes, who like to walk around in long robes, and love greetings in the marketplaces and the best seats in the synagogues and the places of honor at feasts, [47] who devour widows' houses and for a pretense make long prayers. They will receive the greater condemnation."

The Widow's Offering

21 Jesus looked up and saw the rich putting their gifts into the offering box, [2] and he saw a poor widow put in two small copper coins. [3] And he said, "Truly, I tell you, this poor widow has put in more than all of them. [4] For they all contributed out of their abundance, but she out of her poverty put in all she had to live on."

Jesus Foretells Destruction of the Temple

[5] And while some were speaking of the temple, how it was adorned with noble stones and offerings, he said, [6] "As for these things that you see, the days will come when there will not be left here one stone upon another that will not be thrown down."

⁷ And they asked him, "Teacher, when will these things be, and what will be the sign when these things are about to take place?" ⁸ And he said, "See that you are not led astray. For many will come in my name, saying, 'I am he!' and, 'The time is at hand!' Do not go after them. ⁹ And when you hear of wars and tumults, do not be terrified, for these things must first take place, but the end will not be at once."

Jesus Foretells Wars and Persecution

¹⁰ Then he said to them, "Nation will rise against nation, and kingdom against kingdom. ¹¹ There will be great earthquakes, and in various places famines and pestilences. And there will be terrors and great signs from heaven. ¹² But before all this they will lay their hands on you and persecute you, delivering you up to the synagogues and prisons, and you will be brought before kings and governors for my name's sake. ¹³ This will be your opportunity to bear witness. ¹⁴ Settle it therefore in your minds not to meditate beforehand how to answer, ¹⁵ for I will give you a mouth and wisdom, which none of your adversaries will be able to withstand or contradict. ¹⁶ You will be delivered up even by parents and brothers and relatives and friends, and some of you they will put to death. ¹⁷ You will be hated by all for my name's sake. ¹⁸ But not a hair of your head will perish. ¹⁹ By your endurance you will gain your lives.

Jesus Foretells Destruction of Jerusalem

²⁰ "But when you see Jerusalem surrounded by armies, then know that its desolation has come near. ²¹ Then let those who are in Judea flee to the mountains, and let those who are inside the city depart, and let not those who are out in the country enter it, ²² for these are days of vengeance, to fulfill all that is written. ²³ Alas for women who are pregnant and for those who are nursing infants in those days! For there will be great distress

upon the earth and wrath against this people. ²⁴ They will fall by the edge of the sword and be led captive among all nations, and Jerusalem will be trampled underfoot by the Gentiles, until the times of the Gentiles are fulfilled.

The Coming of the Son of Man

²⁵ "And there will be signs in sun and moon and stars, and on the earth distress of nations in perplexity because of the roaring of the sea and the waves, ²⁶ people fainting with fear and with foreboding of what is coming on the world. For the powers of the heavens will be shaken. ²⁷ And then they will see the Son of Man coming in a cloud with power and great glory. ²⁸ Now when these things begin to take place, straighten up and raise your heads, because your redemption is drawing near."

The Lesson of the Fig Tree

²⁹ And he told them a parable: "Look at the fig tree, and all the trees. ³⁰ As soon as they come out in leaf, you see for yourselves and know that the summer is already near. ³¹ So also, when you see these things taking place, you know that the kingdom of God is near. ³² Truly, I say to you, this generation will not pass away until all has taken place. ³³ Heaven and earth will pass away, but my words will not pass away.

Watch Yourselves

³⁴ "But watch yourselves lest your hearts be weighed down with dissipation and drunkenness and cares of this life, and that day come upon you suddenly like a trap. ³⁵ For it will come upon all who dwell on the face of the whole earth. ³⁶ But stay awake at all times, praying that you may have strength to escape all these things that are going to take place, and to stand before the Son of Man."

³⁷ And every day he was teaching in the temple, but at night he went out and lodged on the mount called Olivet. ³⁸ And early in the morning all the people came to him in the temple to hear him.

The Plot to Kill Jesus

22 Now the Feast of Unleavened Bread drew near, which is called the Passover. ² And the chief priests and the scribes were seeking how to put him to death, for they feared the people.

Judas to Betray Jesus

³ Then Satan entered into Judas called Iscariot, who was of the number of the twelve. ⁴ He went away and conferred with the chief priests and officers how he might betray him to them. ⁵ And they were glad, and agreed to give him money. ⁶ So he consented and sought an opportunity to betray him to them in the absence of a crowd.

The Passover with the Disciples

⁷ Then came the day of Unleavened Bread, on which the Passover lamb had to be sacrificed. ⁸ So Jesus sent Peter and John, saying, "Go and prepare the Passover for us, that we may eat it." ⁹ They said to him, "Where will you have us prepare it?" ¹⁰ He said to them, "Behold, when you have entered the city, a man carrying a jar of water will meet you. Follow him into the house that he enters ¹¹ and tell the master of the house, 'The Teacher says to you, Where is the guest room, where I may eat the Passover with my disciples?' ¹² And he will show you a large upper room furnished; prepare it there." ¹³ And they went and found it just as he had told them, and they prepared the Passover.

Institution of the Lord's Supper

¹⁴ And when the hour came, he reclined at table, and the apostles with him. ¹⁵ And he said to them, "I have earnestly desired to eat this Passover with you before I suffer. ¹⁶ For I tell you I will not eat it until it is fulfilled in the kingdom of God." ¹⁷ And he took a cup, and when he had given thanks he said, "Take this, and divide it among yourselves. ¹⁸ For I tell you that from now on I will not drink of the fruit of the vine until the kingdom of God comes." ¹⁹ And he took bread, and when he had given thanks, he broke it and gave it to them, saying, "This is my body, which is given for you. Do this in remembrance of me." ²⁰ And likewise the cup after they had eaten, saying, "This cup that is poured out for you is the new covenant in my blood. ²¹ But behold, the hand of him who betrays me is with me on the table. ²² For the Son of Man goes as it has been determined, but woe to that man by whom he is betrayed!" ²³ And they began to question one another, which of them it could be who was going to do this.

Who Is the Greatest?

²⁴ A dispute also arose among them, as to which of them was to be regarded as the greatest. ²⁵ And he said to them, "The kings of the Gentiles exercise lordship over them, and those in authority over them are called benefactors. ²⁶ But not so with you. Rather, let the greatest among you become as the youngest, and the leader as one who serves. ²⁷ For who is the greater, one who reclines at table or one who serves? Is it not the one who reclines at table? But I am among you as the one who serves.

²⁸ "You are those who have stayed with me in my trials, ²⁹ and I assign to you, as my Father assigned to me, a kingdom, ³⁰ that you may eat and drink at my table in my kingdom and sit on thrones judging the twelve tribes of Israel.

Jesus Foretells Peter's Denial

³¹ "Simon, Simon, behold, Satan demanded to have you, that he might sift you like wheat, ³² but I have prayed for you that your faith may not fail. And when you have turned again, strengthen your brothers." ³³ Peter said to him, "Lord, I am ready to go with you both to prison and to death." ³⁴ Jesus said, "I tell you, Peter, the rooster will not crow this day, until you deny three times that you know me."

Scripture Must Be Fulfilled in Jesus

³⁵ And he said to them, "When I sent you out with no money-bag or knapsack or sandals, did you lack anything?" They said, "Nothing." ³⁶ He said to them, "But now let the one who has a moneybag take it, and likewise a knapsack. And let the one who has no sword sell his cloak and buy one. ³⁷ For I tell you that this Scripture must be fulfilled in me: 'And he was numbered with the transgressors.' For what is written about me has its fulfillment." ³⁸ And they said, "Look, Lord, here are two swords." And he said to them, "It is enough."

Jesus Prays on the Mount of Olives

³⁹ And he came out and went, as was his custom, to the Mount of Olives, and the disciples followed him. ⁴⁰ And when he came to the place, he said to them, "Pray that you may not enter into temptation." ⁴¹ And he withdrew from them about a stone's throw, and knelt down and prayed, ⁴² saying, "Father, if you are willing, remove this cup from me. Nevertheless, not my will, but yours, be done." ⁴³ And there appeared to him an angel from heaven, strengthening him. ⁴⁴ And being in agony he prayed more earnestly; and his sweat became like great drops of blood falling down to the ground. ⁴⁵ And when he rose from prayer, he came to the disciples and found them sleeping for sorrow, ⁴⁶ and

he said to them, "Why are you sleeping? Rise and pray that you may not enter into temptation."

Betrayal and Arrest of Jesus

⁴⁷ While he was still speaking, there came a crowd, and the man called Judas, one of the twelve, was leading them. He drew near to Jesus to kiss him, ⁴⁸ but Jesus said to him, "Judas, would you betray the Son of Man with a kiss?" ⁴⁹ And when those who were around him saw what would follow, they said, "Lord, shall we strike with the sword?" ⁵⁰ And one of them struck the servant of the high priest and cut off his right ear. ⁵¹ But Jesus said, "No more of this!" And he touched his ear and healed him. ⁵² Then Jesus said to the chief priests and officers of the temple and elders, who had come out against him, "Have you come out as against a robber, with swords and clubs? ⁵³ When I was with you day after day in the temple, you did not lay hands on me. But this is your hour, and the power of darkness."

Peter Denies Jesus

⁵⁴ Then they seized him and led him away, bringing him into the high priest's house, and Peter was following at a distance. ⁵⁵ And when they had kindled a fire in the middle of the courtyard and sat down together, Peter sat down among them. ⁵⁶ Then a servant girl, seeing him as he sat in the light and looking closely at him, said, "This man also was with him." ⁵⁷ But he denied it, saying, "Woman, I do not know him." ⁵⁸ And a little later someone else saw him and said, "You also are one of them." But Peter said, "Man, I am not." ⁵⁹ And after an interval of about an hour still another insisted, saying, "Certainly this man also was with him, for he too is a Galilean." ⁶⁰ But Peter said, "Man, I do not know what you are talking about." And immediately, while he was still speaking, the rooster crowed. ⁶¹ And the Lord turned and looked at Peter. And Peter remembered the saying

of the Lord, how he had said to him, "Before the rooster crows today, you will deny me three times." ⁶² And he went out and wept bitterly.

Jesus Is Mocked

⁶³ Now the men who were holding Jesus in custody were mocking him as they beat him. ⁶⁴ They also blindfolded him and kept asking him, "Prophesy! Who is it that struck you?" ⁶⁵ And they said many other things against him, blaspheming him.

Jesus Before the Council

⁶⁶ When day came, the assembly of the elders of the people gathered together, both chief priests and scribes. And they led him away to their council, and they said, ⁶⁷ "If you are the Christ, tell us." But he said to them, "If I tell you, you will not believe, ⁶⁸ and if I ask you, you will not answer. ⁶⁹ But from now on the Son of Man shall be seated at the right hand of the power of God." ⁷⁰ So they all said, "Are you the Son of God, then?" And he said to them, "You say that I am." ⁷¹ Then they said, "What further testimony do we need? We have heard it ourselves from his own lips."

Jesus Before Pilate

23 Then the whole company of them arose and brought him before Pilate. ² And they began to accuse him, saying, "We found this man misleading our nation and forbidding us to give tribute to Caesar, and saying that he himself is Christ, a king." ³ And Pilate asked him, "Are you the King of the Jews?" And he answered him, "You have said so." ⁴ Then Pilate said to the chief priests and the crowds, "I find no guilt in this man." ⁵ But they were urgent, saying, "He stirs up the people, teaching throughout all Judea, from Galilee even to this place."

Jesus Before Herod

⁶ When Pilate heard this, he asked whether the man was a Galilean. ⁷ And when he learned that he belonged to Herod's jurisdiction, he sent him over to Herod, who was himself in Jerusalem at that time. ⁸ When Herod saw Jesus, he was very glad, for he had long desired to see him, because he had heard about him, and he was hoping to see some sign done by him. ⁹ So he questioned him at some length, but he made no answer. ¹⁰ The chief priests and the scribes stood by, vehemently accusing him. ¹¹ And Herod with his soldiers treated him with contempt and mocked him. Then, arraying him in splendid clothing, he sent him back to Pilate. ¹² And Herod and Pilate became friends with each other that very day, for before this they had been at enmity with each other.

¹³ Pilate then called together the chief priests and the rulers and the people, ¹⁴ and said to them, "You brought me this man as one who was misleading the people. And after examining him before you, behold, I did not find this man guilty of any of your charges against him. ¹⁵ Neither did Herod, for he sent him back to us. Look, nothing deserving death has been done by him. ¹⁶ I will therefore punish and release him."

Pilate Delivers Jesus to Be Crucified

¹⁸ But they all cried out together, "Away with this man, and release to us Barabbas"— ¹⁹ a man who had been thrown into prison for an insurrection started in the city and for murder. ²⁰ Pilate addressed them once more, desiring to release Jesus, ²¹ but they kept shouting, "Crucify, crucify him!" ²² A third time he said to them, "Why? What evil has he done? I have found in him no guilt deserving death. I will therefore punish and release him." ²³ But they were urgent, demanding with loud cries that he should be crucified. And their voices prevailed. ²⁴ So Pilate decided that their demand should be granted. ²⁵ He released

the man who had been thrown into prison for insurrection and murder, for whom they asked, but he delivered Jesus over to their will.

The Crucifixion

²⁶ And as they led him away, they seized one Simon of Cyrene, who was coming in from the country, and laid on him the cross, to carry it behind Jesus. ²⁷ And there followed him a great multitude of the people and of women who were mourning and lamenting for him. ²⁸ But turning to them Jesus said, "Daughters of Jerusalem, do not weep for me, but weep for yourselves and for your children. ²⁹ For behold, the days are coming when they will say, 'Blessed are the barren and the wombs that never bore and the breasts that never nursed!' ³⁰ Then they will begin to say to the mountains, 'Fall on us,' and to the hills, 'Cover us.' ³¹ For if they do these things when the wood is green, what will happen when it is dry?"

³² Two others, who were criminals, were led away to be put to death with him. ³³ And when they came to the place that is called The Skull, there they crucified him, and the criminals, one on his right and one on his left. ³⁴ And Jesus said, "Father, forgive them, for they know not what they do." And they cast lots to divide his garments. ³⁵ And the people stood by, watching, but the rulers scoffed at him, saying, "He saved others; let him save himself, if he is the Christ of God, his Chosen One!" ³⁶ The soldiers also mocked him, coming up and offering him sour wine ³⁷ and saying, "If you are the King of the Jews, save yourself!" ³⁸ There was also an inscription over him, "This is the King of the Jews."

³⁹ One of the criminals who were hanged railed at him, saying, "Are you not the Christ? Save yourself and us!" ⁴⁰ But the other rebuked him, saying, "Do you not fear God, since you are under the same sentence of condemnation? ⁴¹ And we indeed justly,

for we are receiving the due reward of our deeds; but this man has done nothing wrong." ⁴²And he said, "Jesus, remember me when you come into your kingdom." ⁴³ And he said to him, "Truly, I say to you, today you will be with me in paradise."

The Death of Jesus

⁴⁴ It was now about the sixth hour, and there was darkness over the whole land until the ninth hour, ⁴⁵ while the sun's light failed. And the curtain of the temple was torn in two. ⁴⁶ Then Jesus, calling out with a loud voice, said, "Father, into your hands I commit my spirit!" And having said this he breathed his last. ⁴⁷ Now when the centurion saw what had taken place, he praised God, saying, "Certainly this man was innocent!" ⁴⁸ And all the crowds that had assembled for this spectacle, when they saw what had taken place, returned home beating their breasts. ⁴⁹ And all his acquaintances and the women who had followed him from Galilee stood at a distance watching these things.

Jesus Is Buried

⁵⁰ Now there was a man named Joseph, from the Jewish town of Arimathea. He was a member of the council, a good and righteous man, ⁵¹ who had not consented to their decision and action; and he was looking for the kingdom of God. ⁵² This man went to Pilate and asked for the body of Jesus. ⁵³ Then he took it down and wrapped it in a linen shroud and laid him in a tomb cut in stone, where no one had ever yet been laid. ⁵⁴ It was the day of Preparation, and the Sabbath was beginning. ⁵⁵ The women who had come with him from Galilee followed and saw the tomb and how his body was laid. ⁵⁶ Then they returned and prepared spices and ointments.

On the Sabbath they rested according to the commandment.

The Resurrection

24 But on the first day of the week, at early dawn, they went to the tomb, taking the spices they had prepared. ² And they found the stone rolled away from the tomb, ³ but when they went in they did not find the body of the Lord Jesus. ⁴ While they were perplexed about this, behold, two men stood by them in dazzling apparel. ⁵ And as they were frightened and bowed their faces to the ground, the men said to them, "Why do you seek the living among the dead? ⁶ He is not here, but has risen. Remember how he told you, while he was still in Galilee, ⁷ that the Son of Man must be delivered into the hands of sinful men and be crucified and on the third day rise." ⁸ And they remembered his words, ⁹ and returning from the tomb they told all these things to the eleven and to all the rest. ¹⁰ Now it was Mary Magdalene and Joanna and Mary the mother of James and the other women with them who told these things to the apostles, ¹¹ but these words seemed to them an idle tale, and they did not believe them. ¹² But Peter rose and ran to the tomb; stooping and looking in, he saw the linen cloths by themselves; and he went home marveling at what had happened.

On the Road to Emmaus

¹³ That very day two of them were going to a village named Emmaus, about seven miles from Jerusalem, ¹⁴ and they were talking with each other about all these things that had happened. ¹⁵ While they were talking and discussing together, Jesus himself drew near and went with them. ¹⁶ But their eyes were kept from recognizing him. ¹⁷ And he said to them, "What is this conversation that you are holding with each other as you walk?" And they stood still, looking sad. ¹⁸ Then one of them, named Cleopas, answered him, "Are you the only visitor to Jerusalem who does not know the things that have happened there in these

days?" ¹⁹ And he said to them, "What things?" And they said to him, "Concerning Jesus of Nazareth, a man who was a prophet mighty in deed and word before God and all the people, ²⁰ and how our chief priests and rulers delivered him up to be condemned to death, and crucified him. ²¹ But we had hoped that he was the one to redeem Israel. Yes, and besides all this, it is now the third day since these things happened. ²² Moreover, some women of our company amazed us. They were at the tomb early in the morning, ²³ and when they did not find his body, they came back saying that they had even seen a vision of angels, who said that he was alive. ²⁴ Some of those who were with us went to the tomb and found it just as the women had said, but him they did not see." ²⁵ And he said to them, "O foolish ones, and slow of heart to believe all that the prophets have spoken! ²⁶ Was it not necessary that the Christ should suffer these things and enter into his glory?" ²⁷ And beginning with Moses and all the Prophets, he interpreted to them in all the Scriptures the things concerning himself.

²⁸ So they drew near to the village to which they were going. He acted as if he were going farther, ²⁹ but they urged him strongly, saying, "Stay with us, for it is toward evening and the day is now far spent." So he went in to stay with them. ³⁰ When he was at table with them, he took the bread and blessed and broke it and gave it to them. ³¹ And their eyes were opened, and they recognized him. And he vanished from their sight. ³² They said to each other, "Did not our hearts burn within us while he talked to us on the road, while he opened to us the Scriptures?" ³³ And they rose that same hour and returned to Jerusalem. And they found the eleven and those who were with them gathered together, ³⁴ saying, "The Lord has risen indeed, and has appeared to Simon!" ³⁵ Then they told what had happened on the road, and how he was known to them in the breaking of the bread.

Jesus Appears to His Disciples

³⁶ As they were talking about these things, Jesus himself stood among them, and said to them, "Peace to you!" ³⁷ But they were startled and frightened and thought they saw a spirit. ³⁸ And he said to them, "Why are you troubled, and why do doubts arise in your hearts? ³⁹ See my hands and my feet, that it is I myself. Touch me, and see. For a spirit does not have flesh and bones as you see that I have." ⁴⁰ And when he had said this, he showed them his hands and his feet. ⁴¹ And while they still disbelieved for joy and were marveling, he said to them, "Have you anything here to eat?" ⁴² They gave him a piece of broiled fish, ⁴³ and he took it and ate before them.

⁴⁴ Then he said to them, "These are my words that I spoke to you while I was still with you, that everything written about me in the Law of Moses and the Prophets and the Psalms must be fulfilled." ⁴⁵ Then he opened their minds to understand the Scriptures, ⁴⁶ and said to them, "Thus it is written, that the Christ should suffer and on the third day rise from the dead, ⁴⁷ and that repentance for the forgiveness of sins should be proclaimed in his name to all nations, beginning from Jerusalem. ⁴⁸ You are witnesses of these things. ⁴⁹ And behold, I am sending the promise of my Father upon you. But stay in the city until you are clothed with power from on high."

The Ascension

⁵⁰ And he led them out as far as Bethany, and lifting up his hands he blessed them. ⁵¹ While he blessed them, he parted from them and was carried up into heaven. ⁵² And they worshiped him and returned to Jerusalem with great joy, ⁵³ and were continually in the temple blessing God.